The Art of Landscape Lighting
A Designer's Companion

JANET LENNOX MOYER FIALD · AOLP · COLD

LONDON AND NEW YORK

Accolades from the Aficionados:

This sumptuous book, lavishly illustrated by George Gruel, provides both a beautiful book just to leaf through, absorbing the beauty of the landscapes, and also a huge educational resource. The inclusion of daylight shots of the lit areas as well as photos of the different seasons and the changes in landscape and planting over many years provides real information that is rarely shared and only otherwise gained over many years of experience and practice. My only worry is that this will exceed the record currently held by Jan Moyer's previous *Landscape Lighting Book* as the one most frequently stolen from my office Library!
—**Kevan Shaw** C. Eng MILP, FIALD, Design Director, Kevan Shaw Lighting Design, Edinburgh, Scotland

Wow! Thank you sooo much for this new, and final book. I think the industry (and everyday people) will benefit greatly from the detail you have gone to in putting this book together. I also love the way the descriptions of each illuminated space are written in mini stories, and also describe your career/life through lighting.
—**Neil Parslow** lightvisuals.co.uk, London, UK

One lighting fixture changed my life! As a person with a disability I spend a lot of time on the couch; at the end of said couch is a window that is dark most evenings. That was until Jan sent me a lighting fixture. Now I look at a maple tree decorated for the seasons: bright red in the Fall; snowy white in the Winter; buds in the Spring; and lush green leaves in the Summer. What was once dark is now light. Jan's breathtaking book illustrates the magic of landscape lighting: whether it is many fixtures illuminating a landscape – or one lighting fixture on a maple tree – Mother Earth is now available year round – how amazing.
—**Catherine Jura** writer, Brunswick, NY

This book is a compendium of Jan's evolution from designer to expert to teacher, and as part textbook and part memoir, allows the reader to understand her growth in skill and sophistication. As a colleague who knows many of the people in her story, especially Michael and George, reading the book is enormously satisfying as much for the story as the result. It is a book to be enjoyed for the dedication of the writer and for her open and honest sharing of a unique and profound career. Not to mention being the best book on landscape lighting one is likely to find on Earth.
—**James R. Benya** PE, FIES, FIALD, Benya Burnett Consultancy, Davis, CA

The Art of Landscape Lighting A Designer's Companion

Following on from the critically acclaimed *The Landscape Lighting Book*, this is the lighting design companion every professional and student in landscape architecture needs. Written by an award-winning internationally renowned landscape lighting designer, with over 40 years' experience in professional practice, *The Art of Landscape Lighting* takes the reader step-by-step through Janet Lennox Moyer's design process.

Personal and accessible in tone, the book covers tools, equipment, techniques, effects, installation, design composition and challenges using built case studies spanning the author's career. Each project takes you through the process of how to plan compositions; selecting what should be lit and what should remain unlit; how to prioritize the importance of multiple elements; balancing brightness relationships; providing visual transportation across scenes; lighting the same space in different ways and, importantly, guidance on when designs are complete.

Lavishly designed and illustrated with 450 full colour photographs, showcasing projects from start to finish, it additionally includes new landscape lighting equipment and techniques developed by Moyer throughout her career. This includes shore scraping, rainwall lighting, approaches for lighting water features and sculptures, and the 3-prong stake.

Aimed at practicing professionals and students in landscape architecture, this book is the must-have inspirational resource that provides you with everything you need to design and implement landscape lighting across multiple scales.

About Janet Lennox Moyer

Janet Lennox Moyer
FIALD, AOLP, COLD, 2018 IES Trailblazer & Icon, 2017 Michigan Lighting Hall of Fame

Jan began her lighting design career in 1976, working on many diverse projects, from the Defense Intelligence Agency's first home in Washington, DC to winery caves, entertainment gardens and botanical gardens. She began specializing in landscape lighting in the mid-1980s and wrote the essential book used around the world, *The Landscape Lighting Book*, first released in 1992 and now in its third edition (John Wiley & Sons), integrating the disruptive technology LED.

Jan began teaching in undergraduate school at Michigan State University, next at the University of Michigan, then at The Academy of Art, SF, UC Berkeley, Rutgers and the Lighting Research Center, among others. She founded The International Landscape Lighting Institute, ILLI, a 501(C)(3) educational non-profit still providing landscape lighting education classes in the US and abroad.

Jan met George Gruel, graphic designer and photographer, in 2004, during the last month of revisions for the second edition of her book. They married in 2005 and George produced a book of Jan's lighting projects, *She Paints with Light*, to help people visualize landscape lighting. Currently Jan is finishing the last of 20 videos for a new educational platform that Garden Light LED is producing with the IESNA called Learn•Night•Light. Jan and George live in Rio Verde, Arizona.

Jan remains committed to sharing her knowledge and striving to raise the bar for the landscape lighting industry, as she would love everyone to be able to enjoy our planet's garden spaces after dark.

Cover Image: George Gruel

First published 2022
by Routledge
4 Park Square, Milton Park, Abingdon, Oxon OX14 4RN

and by Routledge
605 Third Avenue, New York, NY 10158

Routledge is an imprint of the Taylor & Francis Group, an informa business

© 2022 Janet Lennox Moyer

The right of Janet Lennox Moyer to be identified as author of this work has been asserted in accordance with sections 77 and 78 of the Copyright, Designs and Patents Act 1988.

All rights reserved. No part of this book may be reprinted or reproduced or utilised in any form or by any electronic, mechanical, or other means, now known or hereafter invented, including photocopying and recording, or in any information storage or retrieval system, without permission in writing from the publishers.

Trademark notice: Product or corporate names may be trademarks or registered trademarks, and are used only for identification and explanation without intent to infringe.

British Library Cataloguing-in-Publication Data
A catalogue record for this book is available from the British Library

Library of Congress Cataloging-in-Publication Data
Names: Moyer, Janet Lennox, 1954- author. Title: The art of landscape lighting: a designer's companion / Janet Lennox Moyer.

Description: Milton Park, Abingdon, Oxon; New York, NY: Routledge, 2022. | Includes bibliographical references and index. | Identifiers: LCCN 2021050740 (print) | LCCN 2021050741 (ebook) | ISBN 9780367193577 (hardback) | ISBN 9780367193584 (paperback) | ISBN 9780429201882 (ebook)

Subjects: LCSH: Garden lighting. | Landscape architecture. | Exterior lighting.

Classification: LCC SB473.4 .M685 2022 (print) | LCC SB473.4 (ebook) | DDC 621.32/29--dc23/eng/20211208

LC record available at https://lccn.loc.gov/2021050740
LC ebook record available at https://lccn.loc.gov/2021050741

ISBN: 9780367193577 (hbk)

ISBN: 9780367193584 (pbk)

ISBN: 9780429201882 (ebk)

DOI: 10.4324/9780429201882

Typeset in Myriad Pro

Publisher's Note
This book has been prepared from camera-ready copy provided by the author.

Table of Contents
Section I
Learning to Paint with Light
Gathering Tools and Techniques

Once the sun goes down, we lose our connection to our gardens. Landscape lighting can reconnect us by creating an entirely new scene out our windows. This first of four sections introduces the challenges and opportunities that we work with in deciding where and how to paint our garden spaces with light.

I started doing landscape lighting in the 1970's. Not much knowledge had been developed or shared and the actual lighting equipment was limited mostly to 120 volts - there were some 12 volt PAR36 lamps, but with their very narrow beamspreads, they didn't work well for landscape lighting.

Learning how light works takes hours of practice in gardens at night. This book shares what I have learned starting with seeing through our windows that become either black holes or reflections of our interior space. The basic rule is that landscape lighting must balance with interior lighting or be brighter than the room lighting.

If light is introduced into a night space sporadically, there will be too much light, too much light/dark contrast between one element and another, and typically way too much glare. Planning a solid visual composition creates a visual scene that captivates our souls. The relationship of one element and it's brightness to all the others, the brightness hierarchy, provides visual cohesion throughout the garden space(s).

In both small and large garden spaces, providing a visual destination in the distance helps people move through space and understand the space. Typically we need to consider both the vertical and horizontal elements in a space to reveal a comfortable space.

In this Section and Section II I discuss lighting issues for plants, paths/stairs, structures, artwork, and, water features. I also talk about how to bring out the characteristics of a tree; the differences uplighting and downlighting make, and, using both techniques. I identify several issues that result in comfortable and safe walkway and stair lighting. Buildings may or may not deserve lighting and can often be lit by lighting another element, a nearby tree, for example. Many gardens have art and it becomes the focal point. Knowing the art's characteristics and where and how they will be set in a garden is paramount to revealing them with light. Water is the most difficult element that we light, closely followed by fixtures

Learning the Visual Separation of Windows / 1
Planning Visual Composition / 2 – 3
Providing for Visual Cohesion / 4
Lighting a Visual Destination as a Visual Cue / 5
Sculpting Elements
    Trees and Plants / 6 –13
    Paths, Walkways and Stairs / 14 – 16
    Structures / 17 – 19
    Art / 20
    Water/ 21
Creating an Outdoor Room / 22 – 27
Understanding People Moving through Space
    – Physical and Visual / 28
How Light Welcomes Guests / 29 – 30
Seeing the Importance of Shadows / 31

mounted in trees! We need to understand how water and light react and interact with one another. The detailing gets involved to not have glare and to not see fixture cables that distract from the overall lighting effects.

Especially after one and a half years of pandemic, having an outdoor room to enjoy at night increases our enjoyment. These spaces need to be crafted with varying light levels and techniques to create usable, beautiful night rooms.

We need visual information to help us walk through night gardens. The more complicated the space, the more critical the hierarchy of light control. Always including vertical surface lighting will aid our feelings of comfort in the space. Using the brightest light as our visual destination directly relates to how our brain/eye system responds to light.

One of the most important issues at night is welcoming us home or our guests to our home. Using brightness balance throughout a space helps direct us and gives us a sense of the space we are in, so that we can traverse the space with confidence.

I end Section I with using shadows. Creating a lighting scene is always based on light variation and shadows help define, reveal, and play in our night rooms.

Table of Contents
Section II
Design Intuition Takes Over
Honing the Art

Refining and Expanding Design Techniques / 32 – 33
Visual Composition / 34 – 40
View Out a Window / 41 – 42
Planning Movement through Space / 43 – 48
Visual Destination / 49 – 54
Sculpting Elements
    Trees and Plants / 55 – 65
    Paths, Walkways, and Stairs / 66 – 82
    Structures / 83 – 97
    Art / 98 – 101
New Water Technique - Shore Scraping / 102 – 107
Project Challenges
    Rooftops – City HOA and Power Distribution / 108 – 110
    Lighting Long Distances / 111 – 122
    Issues When Lighting a Tight Space / 123 – 128
Radical Landscape Change
    Severe Planting Changes / 129 – 133
    Severe Site Changes / 134 – 143
Respecting the Existing Site / 144 – 153
Snow's Effect on Landscape Lighting / 154 – 162
Renderings - Imagery to Assist Clients to Visualize Your Ideas / 163 – 177
Shadows Define Space - Providing Emphasis or Finesse / 178 – 188

As years flew by I listened to Jackson Browne's' Running on Empty song driving home at 2AM. I realized that landscape lighting is an art. I sent a friend one fixture so she can see a big tree out her window. It makes all the difference in the world to her. Landscape lighting does that.

As I refined my techniques, I honed the visual composition, taking use of the property into account always. Showing the gate to a guest wing entrance to welcome guests. Showing architecture by uplighting trees in front and behind a house, using a higher light level at the back porch as guests spill out of the kitchen.

The experience of every window is different, and, nearly always breath-taking. Even when the lit object is a long distance away or when the effect changes with the seasons.

Movement and visual destination are intrinsically linked. We need to look at the view, think about how someone will feel after dark- if that space isn't lit, and always keep in mind how a garden will change over time. Destinations are not always a place you actually go, sometimes they are visual placeholders, helping us understand and appreciate space.

In the case of Sculpting Elements, my finesse continued to grow as I worked with more and more differing conditions. Time taught me the importance of balancing up and downlighting; how to ensure that all the features of a plant are covered in all seasons; how to gently light stairs and paths so the passing took no thought on the guests' part; for structures, how to show it's strength with understated lighting effect and when the detailing simply deserved highlighting; Detail always makes the composition and if you pay attention, you realize you need a below-grade uplight just for the boar's nose. Water is always the biggest challenge. Developing Shore-scraping, to not miss the connection between water and land, accentuates the reflections and expands the land.

Special situations happen. Roof tops, vast spaces or tight spaces. Paying attention, studying the project documents and working with the team all help you get to solutions for challenging opportunities.

Radical landscape change can take many forms. The big issue about this challenge is planning from the beginning for changes you can't even imagine. I learned to provide extra power and not detail contract documents until we knew the outcome. Snow gives extra emphasis.

Showing a client what they 'could have' became easy once I met George and he did realistic renderings from daytime photos- sometimes even finishing the construction for me. Clients can then make informed decisions about the visual effect they are getting.

Shadows complete a thought – showing the texture of bark on a Willow tree; completing a trees' form by undulating light across a canopy or varying light level on the trunk; revealing the texture on evergreen boughs or stone facades; breaking up a plain wall or endless pavement.

Landscape lighting is passed over by most as simple or not important, but, it holds the key to us enjoying night. We need to pay attention.

Table of Contents
Section III
Not Just Another Light Source
Disruptive Technology Causes New Learning

In the late 1990's LED was starting to storm our planet. It was not ready for landscape lighting. The color was bad, life was brief, output was either way too much or not enough. The electronics people didn't learn lighting and glossed over many important engineering issues - like glare, hiding glare.

In the 2010's additional land made a homes' backyard change completely. With this major change we changed from old technology-halogen light sources to LED. LED offers a color improvement over halogen for plant foliage; it comes to us in broad brush strokes, perfect for landscape lighting. Landscape Lighting manufacturers early on gave us multiple output levels in one fixture, followed by flexible beamspread - no more changing lamps for more/less light or narrower/wider coverage. Interior lighting, today, is still trying to catch up.

One manufacturer has introduced a multi-load, multi-scene controls unit, The Michael System, that changes landscape lighting at whatever rate you choose for 8 hours. While this has been available in theater for years, not in landscape spaces until now.

However, nothing about design changed. Whatever the challenge, we design the same way with a new light source (not the first time, even in my career). As time keeps moving forward the challenges still come and we need to embrace them no matter how we feel about them.

Properties still change and our lighting needs to respond easily.

It doesn't take much light at night to show a space. Our eyes shift to either mesopic or scotopic lighting levels once we step outside, depending on the light level of the neighborhood. In very dark spaces, you can light a really tall tree with a 5-7 watt LED MR16 Flood light source. LED has given us 1/2 watt lamps, 2 watt lamps- many options producing way less light than old technology. That is really valuable in landscape lighting, especially in dark areas. In cities we have to work with the surrounding light level for landscape lighting to show.

Our planet is varied in topography and landscape appearance. Lighting in one area can be completely different than another, often due to native plant palette. Arizona landscapes are less fluffy, more jagged and sharp, and light amazingly. It is different, and we need

My Client Bought the Property Next Door / 189 – 191
Historic Property Gets Sculpture / 192 – 194
Clients Keep Changing Their Art / 195
A Very Quiet Place / 196 – 199
Even More Quiet / 200 – 203
Living Along the Top Edge of a Canyon / 204 – 206
Living In the Sonoran Desert / 207
Rio Verde Community Entrances / 208 – 209
Introducing the Michael System
   by HKusaLighting Group / 210 – 211
Arizona Thrives on Outdoor Living / 212 – 215
Lighting Expands Your Outdoor Living Space / 216 – 220
A Garden for Sculpture / 221 – 223
George Calls it The Last Resort / 224 – 234
Indoor and Outdoor Lighting Can Work Together / 235

to look carefully at differing conditions to understand how to respond with light. Sometimes we softly light a colored wall immediately behind a very strong form cactus – using the age-old silhouette technique that doesn't work in lush East-Coast spaces. Deserts have more open space, which begs us to softly light floor surfaces to help connect areas.

Today, the projects I am working on may be more defined than earlier years. One local project highlights a portion of a clients' art collection; many landscapes have multiple uses. One earlier project had visiting college athletic team practices and political rallies, along with normal uses. Today, many homeowners want multiple seating areas, some with fire pits and all the bells and whistles available; some gardens have multiple areas with differing style or usage. Gardens are used and enjoyed more.

We need to be cognizant of all the changes that will continue to occur in garden spaces. Plants get added or die, people add or change spaces, art and waterfeatures are introduced or moved!.We need to produce as-built documents that aid us in small or big renovations.

Table of Contents
Section IV
The International Landscape Lighting Institute
Teaching via the Intensive Course

Explaining the Intensive Course / 236 – 245
Design Teams Need to Work Together / 246 – 247
Groups of Trees Create a Night Space / 248 – 255
Saluki Park Mockup Areas
- **Lighting the Pond / 256 – 264**
- **Lighting the Birch Grove / 265 – 269**
- **Lighting the Forests / 270 – 279 Lighting the Black Walnuts / 280 – 285 Lighting Individual Conifers / 286 – 287 Lighting the Beech Trees / 288 – 293 Lighting the Apple Orchard / 294 – 297 Lighting the Oaks and Maples / 298 – 303**

Mockups and Installations
- **Brunswick, New York / 304 – 319**
- **Rio Verde, Arizona 2015 & 2019 / 320 – 325**
- **Ridgewood, New Jersey 2016 / 326 – 331**
- **Tokamachi, Japan 2017 / 332 – 344**
- **ILLI Class Photos / 345 – 347**

A Vintage, Intensive Course, Flyer / 348

After sharing my lighting knowledge for years not enough people understood the intricacies of imagining, installing, the final design involved in aiming, and the maintenance required to keep a system looking right. After writing *The Landscape Lighting Book*, to share lighting knowledge, I then embarked on creating an international educational foundation to help raise the level of understanding and design possible for lighted spaces.

The Landscape Lighting Institute (ILLI) offers a 5-day, 4 night immersion course with lectures, demonstrations, and an attendee-team full scale mockup project. Often called lighting 'boot camp', attendees have the opportunity to work with nearly all manufacturers fixtures and try any ideas they have wondered about. Throughout the process, teams of 5 attendees are guided by a team of three mentors, who earlier graduated from the course. On the last night, the teams present their designs to the public- honing their marketing skills.

Over the years, George recorded all the efforts and rewards, amassing a treasure trove of photos, showing varying design ideas for the same areas. While all the mockups were temporary, finished for one nights' enjoyment, this collection shows how lighting can sculpt space for our personal use. From the apple orchard to expansive areas around the main house, and the entrance to Georges' remote studio, ideas abound for all possibilities.

Lighting for the same space planned by different design teams illustrates varying ways to render the same space with different intentions.

I show multiple areas to expand on how different designers, taking the same space, make completely different visual compositions. Discussing each areas issues and challenges, along with teams design intents, these pages show many ways spaces can be crafted to reveal stunning night rooms and experiences. At the pond, sometimes reflecting the night scene in the waters' surface, other times integrating the waters changing edge of reeds develops completely different imagery/experience.

Trees vary and understanding their characteristics from overall form to how their leaves interact with light shows a designer how to bring out the intrinsic beauty of any tree, even a mishapped one, using light. Page after page shows comparisons of treatments, including the amazing effect snow adds to a lit scene.

Creating these mockups courses takes an inordinate amount of pre-planning, effort during the course by the design teams, and reorganizing afterwords for the next set of designers. It takes commitment of a massive team of mentors, well over 100 now that continue offering this amazing opportunity, essentially to our competitors!

Over the years, ILLI took the opportunity to create permanent installations so that from New York to Japan, there are places people can walk through parks to experience amazing lighting. Through the course content, these installations are done by multiple designers. Starting with 10 mentor teams creating ten residential 'rooms' people could walk through and see, experience, what lighting offers night spaces. The parks conditions and planting varied with their location including a hillside park in downtown Ridgewood, NY, a desert park in Rio Verde, AZ and culminating at a park in Tokamachi, Japan along the Kiyotsugawa River.

Acknowledgments

I call this book a 'companion.' It culminates the sharing I started when I was still a college student. Even at that time, so many people shared with me, and guided my movement into adulthood. I have never stopped sharing my knowledge and experience, and with this book I feel that professionally I can be done. A new client said that he hoped I would want to photograph his project when we are done. I knew that the project we photographed the previous week for this book could be my last. This book allows me to show everyone how lighting gives you a surrounding of art at night. This book gives all that I wasn't able to give in the three editions of *The Landscape Lighting Book*, completing what I can offer to you.

I need to thank each and every client that I have designed lighting for over the last 45 years. Their projects gave me the opportunity and challenges that fill the pages of this book and have filled my landscape lighting tool box with all the incredible night art we created together.

The list of comrades that have worked on making those projects create beautiful night scenes is a long one, and, I fear that I have forgotten some. Many design assistants have helped me get documents produced and spent nights in the field creating the lighting scenes that I envision. At this age many names are lost to me, but the time together still warms my heart.

So many people gave their all, as students, contractors, and designers, work with me on sites night after night to make our projects great starting with Dave Edwards, Mark Schulkamp, David Brearey, Don Bradley, Tony Lato, John Kenney, Ken Martin, Jesse Loucks, Paul Randolph, Sr, Richard Vargas, Kirk Bianchi, Emery Rogers, David Kelly, Matt Jarrett, Shane O'Keeffe, Dan Dyer, Jessica Collier, Kathleen Toth, Karen Libby, & Andy Robbins.

Next, I need to thank each and every person that has participated in The International Landscape Lighting Institute – to this day, several years after I gave up leading it. I am still learning about landscape lighting from all that we do together.

I need to thank my original editor, Grace Harrison, my current editor, Kathryn Schell, and her editorial assistant, Sean Speers for their guidance and support in getting this to the finish line.

More than anyone, I need to thank George Gruel, my amazing husband. He took my interest in both landscape and landscape lighting to heart; he is my 'plant enabler' as he takes me to amazing gardens, nurseries and plant sales, and even finds plants he wants to bring home. Early in our friendship, he asked if he could photograph my gardens and my projects. George honed landscape lighting photography to an art extraordinaire. He has laid out this entire book and patiently assisted me in every crisis to make this the best that we can.

Michele Lott spent hours scouring for grammatical issues. I cannot thank her enough for helping get this work cleaned up and ready for you to read.

This being my last book, I want to dedicate it to all the dogs that have supported me emotionally, begging me to come out and play when I was stressed – Sashee, Killy, Kona, Kabuki, Gerenuk, Two, Tigger, Travis, Pierre, Potatoh, Jackioh, Uncle Nephew, Sunshine and Ahmar.

Preface

Getting the call from Grace Harrison inquiring if I would consider writing a full-color book on landscape lighting lured me back into writing. To really experience lighting, you have to be in the space, but the next best thing is to look at color photographs of lighting. Now we will have it, thanks to Grace and Routledge.

This book is four sections with the first being the time period, when I lived in California and spent 4 or 5 nights each week working into the wee morning hours, and then still worked nearly normal office hours, day after day. I couldn't get enough time with lighting equipment in the dark during those 20 or so years. My neighbors let me do mock-ups in their yards to expand my knowledge and understanding of what light can bring to our space. This is the section where I share what I learned, in those early mockups, and how I applied it to projects.

Section II includes the time that I created non-stop. Honing every technique I had learned, creating new techniques, and better understanding how to design and document for the future maintenance and project expansions to come. While teaching both at UC Berkeley and Rutgers, a student's comment challenged me to study how snow affects and interacts with landscape lighting – something very important for many areas of planet Earth. George showed me how we could easily show my vision to clients across the country by using photography and graphic design to produce digital imagery of the clients lighting. Michael Hookers' saying that "Darkness is your friend" stayed in my head and my heart while I played with the darkness that shadows add to lighting scenes.

Then came the time, about 2009, when LED lamps were actually starting to have adequate color rendering and enough light output to consider using them in landscape lighting. There were many other considerations to ponder when deciding whether to jump into LED use (covered in the 3rd edition of *The Landscape Lighting Book*). Moving away from old technology to LED became a whole new learning era. Simply changing out wattage and beam-spread did not create an acceptable change to existing halogen lighting projects. Rather, it's like learning a new language. The tools appear to be the same, but the way they perform is vastly different. In this last era of my career, I am still working throughout this country and the world, but lighting in the desert is so different.

The third section shows specific learning issues, some included in earlier sections, but here with different challenges to share: big site changes, art and more art in the garden, Living in the Sonoran Desert with the challenges and opportunities extreme environments present. Each expanding how we can continue to let the darkness we experience every night be beautiful and livable.

Section IV explains how The International Landscape Lighting Institute, the educational nonprofit that I founded, still today offers an incredible learning experience. This section shows and compares what we need to think about in multiple landscape settings, with multiple types of trees and varying types of scenes or installations. The wealth of ideas, techniques, and compositions that a multitude of attendees, IALD funded students, design professionals of all kinds and a smattering of normal people from nurses to lighting manufacturers, pilots to astrophysicists experimented with shows us unlimited ways that we can approach the night environment. And, where the line is between many good approaches to that line where light becomes too much.

This book is full of night scenes of all kinds that professionals and homeowners can use as a guide to help them understand the possibilities for their nighttime outdoor living spaces. Enjoy!

Photograph and Art Credits

David Brearey, PhD,
Hill Road Lighting, hillroadlighting.com
davidbrearey@icloud.com
Page 162

Daniel L. Dyer,
dyerdrpi@gmail.com
Pages 55, 102, 259, 260

George Gruel,
OddStick Studio, oddstick.com, gruel@mac.com, 518-470-3620
Pages 2, 3, 16, 21, 24 -29, 32-33, 34-45, 46-69, 70-75,7 7-82, 86-89, 91-97, 98-101, 103-107, 108-110, 112, 115-119, 120-123, 125-126, 128-130, 133,137, 141,1 48-154, 156-159, 161, 163-188, 236-256, 261-264, 266-269, 272-279, 281-284, 286-300, 302-317, 320-326, 328-341, 343-344

Patrick Harders,
Sterling Lighting, patrick@sllights.com, 800-939-1849
Pages 327, 347

HK Lighting Group,
Hklightinggroup.com, 802-480-4881
Pages 71, 342-343

Hollander Design Landscape Architects,
astrickler@hollanderdesign.com, 312-523-6569
Page 123

Anthony Lato,
well_lit_llc@mac.com, 203-515-9650
Page 99

Greg Matthews,
Luxury Illumination. Greg@luxuryillumination.net, 516-644-3860
Pages 324-325, 347

Janet Lennox Moyer and Jan Moyer Design,
janmoyerdesign@mac.com, 518-573-9753
Pages 2, 4-7, 9-10, 13-22, 24, 26, 28, 34, 36, 39, 41, 43, 51-53, 55-58, 62-64, 67-68, 70-73, 76, 81-82, 84-87, 90, 92, 95, 102, 110-111, 113-115, 117, 119-121, 123-124, 126-129, 131-132, 134-140, 142, 144-145, 148, 151, 154-155, 158-161, 165, 167, 170-172, 188, 196, 231, 236-237, 240, 256-259, 265, 270-271, 280, 285-289, 294, 301, 304, 308-309, 318-319, 345

Mary E. Nichols,
Mary E. Nichols Photography, maryenicholsphotography.com,
mary@maryenicholsphotography.com, 323-424-7889
Pages xiii &1

Kenneth Rice,
Kenneth Rice Photography, kenricephotopeoplecom,
kenricephoto@aol.com
Pages 4-8, 10, 11-13, 14, 16-18, 20-23, 25, 28, 30-33, 142, 144, 155, 160, 180, 182-183

Doug Salin,
Douglas A. Salin Photography,
doug@dougsalin.com, 415-584-3322
Pages 6, 15, 29

Kevin Simonson,
kevin@atthetabernacle.com
Pages 158, 160, 284, 286, 301

Tom Williams,
Williams Lighting Design
Pages 146, 147

2012-2013 Landscape Lighting Exhibiton Teams

Area A: Manufacturer, Lumiere, Cooper Lighting Solutions, cooperlighiting.com
Design Team: Betsy Mitchell, John Kenny, Rick Dekeyser

Area B: Manufacturer, HK Lighting Group, hklightinggroup.com, Anna Cheng, Reiko Kido, and Satoshi Suzuki
Design Team: Kathryn Toth, Andy Robbins, Heinrich Fischer

Area C: Manufacturer, Vision 3 Lighting, vision3lighting.com
Design Team: Emily Gorecki, Jesse Loucks, Jim Ply

Area D: Manufacturer, Kichler Lighting, kichler.com
Design Team: David Brearey, Kyle Eddie

Area E: Manufacturer, Cast Lighting, cast-lighting.com, Duncan Fuller
Design Team: John Pletcher, Brooke Silber, Bill Smith

Area F: Manufacturer, Excelsior Lighting, Jerry Carter
Design Team: Kristy Benner, Lara Cordell Ken Martin, Jon Carlo Marras, Greg Yale

Area G: Manufacturer, FX Luminaire, fxl.com, Tom Marmestein, Kris Klein
Design Team: Brooke Perin, Oscar Welch, Paul Welty

Area H: Manufacturer, BK Lighting
Design Team: Don Bradley, Marilyn Schultz-Goldfine, Ken Simons

Area I: Manufacturer, Beachside Lighting, beachsidelighting.com, Rick Benedict
Design Team: Pam Bingham, Chris Mitchell, Tom Williams

Area J: Manufacturer, CooperMoon, coopermoon.com
Design Team: Jen Brons, Tony Lato, Mike Nantz

Other Credits

Book Layout and Design: George Gruel

Front and Back Cover Design, Layout and Photos: George Gruel

Proofreading and Design Guide: Michele Lott

Reviews: James R. Benya, Catherine Jura, Neil Parslow, Kevan Shaw

The tree ferns are uplit with stake mount fixtures located on the window side of the plants, to a high light level as art seen from the kitchen. This avoids reflections or a dark hole and finishes the room.

SECTION 1
Learning to Paint with Light
Gathering Tools and Techniques
Learning the Visual Separation of Windows

This living room in the Berkeley Hills in California was one of my early experiences. My mentor, Fran Kellogg Smith, accompanied me to the site and then wanted me to do the design on my own. The job was to light this living room, but look at those windows! Everything those windows saw had to be included or my design would not work. My landscape lighting career began in this room and it ignited my passion for landscape lighting.

At this site I learned a the basic rule we all need to understand about light and its interaction with glass. Interior light levels are significantly higher than outdoor levels. To avoid reflection, when looking from a room out into a garden, the objects lit outside need to be at least as bright as inside objects. In the lower left photo the reflections on the glass wall from the opposite window show. When you look carefully at the upper night image, you may see the reflection in the window of the rounded decorative fixture just above the piano. Putting light onto glass does not mitigate reflections.

I lit the sculpture at the end of the walkway, as the focal object providing visual destination. The plantings are lit with both stake mount uplights and building mounted downlights. By uniformly uplighting the ceiling plane, cross-lighting from the cove, you may not notice the reflection of that architectural feature in the window.

Learning to Paint with Light *Gathering Tools and Techniques*
SECTION I
Planning Visual Composition

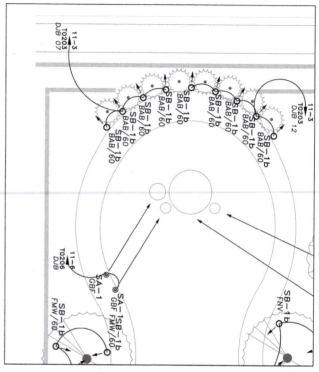

This garden in Northern CA has a formal layout along the entry walk. Uplighting the fruit trees frames the scene. Grazing the hedge behind the sculpture provides a backdrop and a visual end-point. Making the sculpture the focal point are two stake mount uplights and two eave mounted downlights – arrows in the above drawing show how the lights are aimed to bring out the form and texture of the four elements.

I left the bottom of the hedge dark, up to just above the sculpture for separation. The eave lights have the inside of their angled glare shields painted flat black to minimize light flash-back onto the house. These were done on site by the contractor with high-heat spray paint. Many manufacturers will do it at the factory.

Gathering Tools and Techniques **Learning to Paint with Light**
SECTION I

Planning Visual Composition

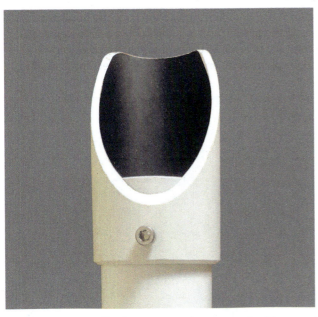
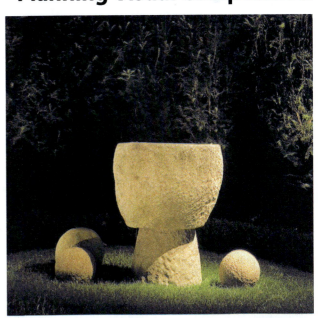

Gardens continually change over the years – in this case, the fruit trees were replaced with Olive trees. It was about the time that I felt comfortable to start retrofitting existing projects with LED. This was early on in LED replacement lamp development so the lamps were not yet stable.

The new LED lamps create a different feeling in the space. We used the same fixture layout with 3000°K LED lamps producing a more vibrant green foliage. Another difference using LED is that beam spreads are much wider making the effects wider. The separation made by leaving the lower hedge dark for the sculpture is gone.

Probably 10-15 years after the initial lighting installment, this softer overall lighting provides the 'dreamy' effect for which we used to rely on halogen's color.

Learning to Paint with Light *Gathering Tools and Techniques*
SECTION I

Providing for Visual Cohesion

It gets dark every night. We hold the keys to creating the magic of chasing darkness away. We have the opportunity to carefully craft visual scenes out of the darkness. We can recreate the garden as it is in daylight or select elements to highlight and/or others to hide. In this process, we need to carefully provide visual cohesion across the scene. By balancing brightness and thinking about the relationship from one element to another, the scene becomes visually stable and comfortable for us at night.

In the photo above, the arbor, the hedge behind the stage and the big trees on the right are all similar in their apparent brightness. This provides 'visual transportation' across the scene. Downlighting provides a natural appearance. Fixtures mounted in the Redwood tree downlight the top of the greenhouse structure, the planting bed in front of the greenhouse, the planting bed to the left of the water feature, and the stage/balustrade. The right tree has a downlight fixture grazing the top of the hedge, photo above, bottom right corner.

For the fountain to be the focal point, it needs to be a minimum of three times brighter than the surrounding elements. To make that happen, I decided to leave the pool and the lawn dark. That darkness increases the perception of the brightness of the fountain.

This garden space in Northern CA is formally balanced from left to right. On the left, the arbor and the greenhouse are far larger than the planting beds both left and right of the lawn. At first glance, you would think that you could put lights into those two beds, however, plantings are completely changed at least four times a year. No fixtures could hold their aim with that much activity around them.

The big Redwood tree, back left, provides downlighting for several elements in the scene, as does the trellis, just visible at the bottom right.

Gathering Tools and Techniques **Learning to Paint with Light**
SECTION I

Lighting a Visual Destination as a Visual Cue

Throughout this book you will see I start my thinking with downlighting. It gently lights more area, isn't knocked out of adjustment by tools, or grown over by ground covers. It holds the lighting effects much longer than uplights, and appears more natural as we are familiar with that direction of light from the sun in the daytime.

This client called me one day and said how lucky she felt to come home each night to experience this lighting. Her family dining table looked out on this arbor. I tucked pairs of stake mount uplights into the hedge flanking the path. They are aimed at about 15° to highlight the curve of the structure and graze the Potato vine and Roses all the way to the greenhouse. That limited aiming angle and a honeycomb louver stopped any glare as someone walked along the walk, and no pathlights are needed.

At the end, I downlit the greenhouse roof from the Redwood tree and uplit ground plantings in front of the greenhouse, giving the scene a visual destination.

5

Learning to Paint with Light *Gathering Tools and Techniques*
SECTION I
Sculpting Elements – Trees and Plants

To show three dimensional characteristics of a tree requires fixtures around the canopy – typically, a minimum of three. This tree, Lagerstroemia indica/Crape Myrtle, flowers on the ends of its branches at a time when most other trees are not blooming, requiring fixtures outside the canopy.

This tree has been pruned, lifting the canopy and exposing the trunks. The bark on the trunk is mottled, creating patterns. This tree taught me that I need to pay attention to tying the tree canopy to the ground by lighting the trunk and branching structure.

The similar brightness of the step lighting, the tree trunks, and the pool sculptures visually links all these Northern CA backyard elements. Notice the grazing effect on the far hedging plants that provides a sense of the end for the space.

This young tree, left/above, has a much tighter, lower canopy. It will open up as it matures, but pruning will be necessary to make sense of the branching pattern.

Gathering Tools and Techniques **Learning to Paint with Light**
SECTION I

Sculpting Elements – Trees and Plants

We don't normally pay attention to how long some conifer branches are even though we look right at them every day. Lighting can emphasize that trait showing their majestic size. At right, the light fixture for the right tree is about 20' away from it, so it is not grazing but washing that tree, even though it looks like grazing. In this Northern CA property the Crabapples show my first attempt at downlighting to show ground plane. After seeing this effect, I knew I had to fix it by softening the output and widening the beam spreads.

The Quercus agrifolia/California Live Oak below has three uplights showing its trunk and branching pattern, with one downlight for the lower branch and one for the bench. Look closely and you'll see that the outer canopy is dark, so the neighbors don't see any lighting from their property.

Learning to Paint with Light *Gathering Tools and Techniques*
SECTION I
Sculpting Elements – Trees and Plants

These Apple trees in a Northern CA project taught me the importance of thinking from one season to another, how to uplight canopies for both summer and winter, and to look at the trees form to decide how to light its various trunks.

Notice all the water sprouts going straight up out of the canopy in the lower photo. We had those pruned off before winter when the leaves are gone showing the branching structure in the photo at left.

Multiple uplights are positioned under the canopy to show its form. Not all are the same brightness, treating it as a sculptural element and creating its night-time appearance. From summer to winter that sculpting remains, just less prominent in the summer with the leaves filling the canopy.

The amount of light and position of fixtures is critical. A light right underneath the branch, as you see with the largest branch on the right side, becomes the strongest brightness, summer and winter.

Putting a light under a low branch is often a problem and most times we want to avoid a light right under a branch.

These apples, sentimental to the owners, were an important part of the view from their back deck. As a team we chose to put downlights in the Apples to provide downlighting of the shrubs planted under the trees.

Downlighting provides a sense of reality to a scene no matter how dramatic, like this one. Without the downlighting, the drama would be much bolder and the trees would be on a dark stage.

Notice that you don't see the fixtures in the canopy, summer or winter. Working hard with the installing contractor, we determined locations that provided the lighting effect I wanted and did not show – either day or night. This kind of care in approaching any tree, creates the artistic appearance you see here.

Gathering Tools and Techniques **Learning to Paint with Light**
SECTION I

Sculpting Elements – Trees and Plants

These two photos show how we ran the wire on the 'backside' of trees (Crabapple, left and Apple, right) – you can see the viewing direction from the deck at right in the right image. As you learn in *The Landscape Lighting Book*, I use eyelet cable ties for attaching the cable along the trunk or branch – so that the cable is not actually attached, but is held in place. We want the screws to have threads showing, and, know the growth rate of the tree to determine the timing for backing-off the screws due to growth. It varies between one kind of tree and another, and, between young and mature trees, but, for many tree species, it isn't that frequent, typically from once a year to once over multiple years.

Remember that the fixture will always stay at its initial location. Branches grow in length from their tips, so fixtures don't move, but trunks and branches also expand in width as they grow. We need to provide spare cable at the base of the tree to accommodate that horizontal expansion growth.

Looking closely at these two images, you will see that I have the angled glare shields located to shield view into the fixture from the house. Both of these images show you the effect from the side, allowing you to see the cable run and both fixture/glare shield positioning. Also, notice how I have located the mounting canopies on the back side of the branch to help minimize any view of the fixture. In the left photo, the fixture in between the branches is aimed back toward the house. It is so close to the branch that, without the uplighting, the effect on the tree may be too bright.

Having learned early on the benefit of mounting fixtures in trees to light the tree itself or light something below it, either softly or as a focal element, I discovered the lasting effect and the width of coverage possible from a tree mounted fixture – a major technique in our lighting tool box.

Learning to Paint with Light *Gathering Tools and Techniques*
SECTION I

Sculpting Elements – Trees and Plants

Trees vary so much in their growth habit and appearance characteristics that I study them to understand how they will change over time as they mature. These are the first Sequoia sempervirens/Redwood trees I lit. They are dense, tall trees creating a lot of shadows during the day with a little sunlight coming through where it can. As with many projects, we had a limited budget, and I could only use one fixture per tree and none for some trees. Below, you can see that a view through this Redwood forest to the side of this home gave us a surprise view to a palm tree... not expected with Redwoods.

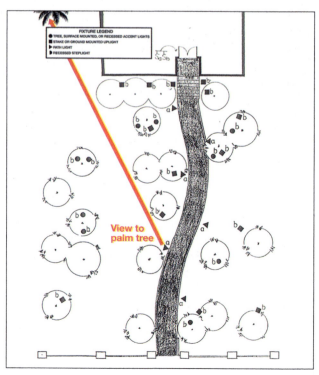

Gathering Tools and Techniques **Learning to Paint with Light**
SECTION I

Sculpting Elements – Trees and Plants

Above, you can see that Redwood trunks are tall – they can reach over 350'/111.5 meters, naturally sloughing lower branches over time.

To light this grove in Northern CA, for arriving guests and for the view from the dining room window, I needed a lamp that could throw strong light up roughly 100'/30m. While Halogen MR16 lamps had just become available (mid-1980s), I needed a PAR38 Halogen lamp with a strong enough spot to reach the height and with enough spill between one tree's canopy and another's to fill across the grove.

Fixtures that hold PAR38 lamps are much bigger than the smaller fixtures we like to use to easily hide in landscape spaces. In this situation today I would avoid using LED retrofit lamps, and use an integral module LED fixture designed to have enough candlepower to get to that extreme height. Some manufacturers now offer multiple output or integral fixture output adjustment. It doesn't take much light for most trees. In 2021, I typically use less than 10 watts to get to the top of most trees canopies, including these Redwoods.

Learning to Paint with Light *Gathering Tools and Techniques*
SECTION I
Sculpting Elements – Trees and Plants

The location of a tree will direct how you light it. This Acer japonicum/Full Moon Maple sat right in front of the front door of this Northern CA home, meaning it could not be the focal point of the lighting for this front garden, even though it was the star specimen tree – planted some 30+ years ago when we lit it. The branching structure is beautiful and a strong element of the tree. Its canopy is full and rounded with typical diaphanous Maple leaves and many openings, so it is not a dense canopy. I wanted to show the overall canopy, but not distract guests from finding the front door (see p14). Looking at the drawing on the next page, I used three fixtures for the canopy and two for the trunk. You may think that is a lot of fixtures, but it has a 30' spread and the view of the trunk is important from the front door as guests leave, as well as from the gate when they arrive. There is one downlight mounted on the adjacent trellis for the ground plane when you are inside the brick wall.

Gathering Tools and Techniques **Learning to Paint with Light**
SECTION I

Sculpting Elements – Trees and Plants

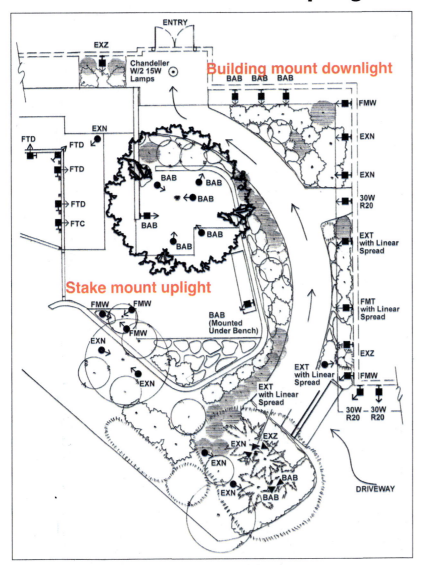

From the front door, one of the two trunk uplights is behind on the left creating a strong edge-light effect. It needs the soft wash from the fixture on the right side to soften the overall effect.

Having been done in the 1980s, it feels too bright to me now. I would light the tree and all the elements in this garden at a lower light level today, still being careful to keep the balance of brightness from one part of the tree to another, and from one element in the scene to another as you see here.

As this would be an existing project when LED became available, if I were to retrofit this I would use LED replacement lamps to convert it. When you do that, you save between 70-90% of the electrical load.

For new projects, I would design this using integral module fixtures, if the budget allowed. Many manufacturers offer flexible beam spread and dimming right at the fixture to create exactly the effects desired – ahead of the dimming system.

Learning to Paint with Light *Gathering Tools and Techniques*
SECTION I
Sculpting Elements – Paths, Walkways, and Stairs

In the daytime photo above looking straight to the front door, part of the Maple canopy is visible, while at night you see the trunk and most of the canopy. It is important to help guests find their way along a path from where they park at night. The front door should be the brightest element. In the before photo, lower left, you can see the front door but not necessarily recognize it as such, and, with all that darkness between you and that door, the walk is not comfortable. Before the new lighting, I lamped and aimed the existing lighting the best I could, but compared with the 'new' 1990s lighting (above right), it would not be comfortable to navigate. With the eave downlighting, seen in the drawing on p13, and tree downlighting along the left side of the walk to the brick wall, the walk becomes clear and easily navigated. On the right side of the walk is a long garage wall. I introduced shadowing on the wall to make it more interesting at night.

Gathering Tools and Techniques **Learning to Paint with Light**
SECTION I

Sculpting Elements – Paths, Walkways, and Stairs

I uplit the 'Crimson Queen Maple' on one side to create the shadow patterns on the large expanse of wall and downlit it on the other side, to balance the tree's appearance. Lighting vertical elements in a space and identifying the boundaries increases a sense of comfort for people at night, especially in unfamiliar spaces.

I will do back flips to avoid using pathlights. They don't add to the aesthetic appearance of a garden. Yet there are many spaces that require them where downlighting from a building or tree cannot be done. The upper left photo shows a completely shielded, forward-throw path light. I have put it right at the intersection of two steps to increase its coverage. At the right I put these completely shielded historical-looking fixtures (to blend with the historical architecture) with tall stems among taller plantings back away from the path, probably about 18'/.5m high, letting the light fall onto the lower path side plantings and onto the path iself.

It is important to understand that as vertical beings, we see vertical surfaces before we see horizontal ones, so lighting walls, trees, sculptures, water features, any vertical elements around us helps us feel comfortable in dark spaces. Typically, paths and walkways are the least important visual element in a night landscape, if there are no steps. While they are important to see and navigate, when the site doesn't have steps or other obstacles (which could even be a kids' bike dropped while running home for dinner), other elements are more important to our understanding of the space and our feeling of safety in a space.

Later in the book, I will show examples of lighting stairs more in-depth. For now, think about the intersection of the riser and the tread – that is the key element to show. Limiting shadows at that intersection point helps people understand the stairs, especially older people. The more uneven or unusual the stairs' layout, the more attention is required to provide better lighting for people to navigate them comfortably. Notice I did not say 'more' light. Since our minds can fill in it simply does not take much light so we don't have to evenly light stairs or light them all the way across their width for people to feel comfortable in a dark unfamiliar space.

Learning to Paint with Light *Gathering Tools and Techniques*
SECTION I
Sculpting Elements – Paths, Walkways, and Stairs

Walking along an uneven set of stones to a step that is unusually high before reaching the door would be uncomfortable at night without lighting that reveals the unevenness. Downlighting from the overhangs is aimed onto the plantings and spills onto the stones and the step. I don't locate or aim fixtures at the middle of a path, as that light above our heads is uncomfortable. Light grazing the texture of this door makes it even more intriguing at night.

At lower left, the daytime photo of the path shows the walkway, but not the pot at the end. Downlighting from the eaves of this house aims the main candlepower onto plantings across the walk with light spilling onto the path and clearly showing the pot at the end.

Gathering Tools and Techniques **Learning to Paint with Light**
SECTION I

Sculpting Elements – Structures

Lighting this lath house (1980s), I learned that you don't actually have to light the structure to have it show clearly at night. Overhead lighting inside the lath house shows the cactus collection and provides a clear view into the space. The structure is shown through a combination of uplights for lighting plants within, downlights for lighting plants around the structure, and by that interior lighting.

Adding an angled glare shield, similar to the one on page 3, blocks your eye from seeing the inside of the downlights. While they are only aimed about 20° above zenith, in the upper right photo you see the inside of the fixture. That is the brightest element and it will always be in a landscape. It distracted one from the scene, until a few years later I convinced the manufacturer to make an angled glare shield that fits over the fixture, at right.

Learning to Paint with Light *Gathering Tools and Techniques*
SECTION I
Sculpting Elements – Structures

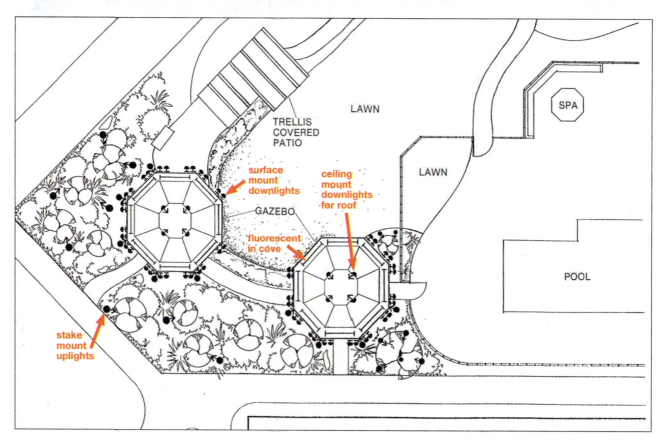

Gathering Tools and Techniques **Learning to Paint with Light**
SECTION I

Sculpting Elements – Structures

This is another early example of lighting from inside and around the building, using the structure as a mounting location. I continue to do that over the years, but will show other techniques later on as well.

For this Northern CA retirement community the owner created a series of garden spaces throughout the property and linked them with walkways and these gathering pavilions. She wanted her residents to get out and spend time with each other. The pavilions have indirect fluorescent cove lighting, enough light for the residents to play cards and other games, or simply chat with a glass of wine.

Using the pavilion as a mounting location, we grouped four fixtures at each corner. This allowed us to light plantings around the buildings to increase the resident's sense of comfort. In some cases these fixtures lit the entrances to the pavilions.

Transformers are recessed in a plenum-like open space at the edges of the pavilion. We provided hatches for access to the transformers for maintenance. Having them so close allowed us to limit voltage drop around the pavilion, a problem with old technology as voltage reduces quickly at 12 volts.

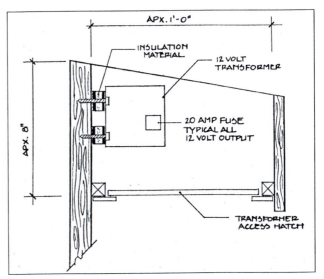

I want everyone to remember that voltage drop is still a real issue with our new LED technology. The electrical runs now can be much longer than for old technology, but voltage drop still can become an issue if you don't plan it well. It is always best to have a 120-volt source as close to your load as possible and for all futures loads, known and unknown. During construction provide power distribution to remote parts of the site to be prepared for lighting.

Transformers hum and the sound gets exaggerated on many materials, wood being one of them. We mounted the transformers on the wooden surface with small pieces of Korfund isolating material. It consists of two layers of elastomeric pad with horizontal ribs on one side and vertical on the other, with cork in between. While I couldn't find this product now, other dampening materials should be available.

Because we had the 'plenum' space, it allowed us to use flat-mounting plates for each fixture slightly reducing the size of the fixture. You will note that you can see brightness from the inside of all the fixtures. I don't recall why we don't have glare shields – they would help.

Learning to Paint with Light *Gathering Tools and Techniques*
SECTION I
Sculpting Elements – Art

Art is a frequently used element in outdoor spaces. I learned early on to provide power in the vicinity of the art placement in the garden, but not committing to how to light the piece until it is in place.

The monkey statue above is a good example. I had to move the downlight that keys-in on his headdress, face, and shoulders about 3 feet to keep the eyes from being in shadow.

With the piece 'Dante's Dream of an Eagle' by Harriet Moore (upper left), I spoke with her about the sculpture first and then chose to spot light the two heads, the man, and the eagle. The shadow on the wall was a surprise which taught me how we can use one fixture to provide more than one effect. A red gel allows the fire of hell to speak for itself.

When sculptures move, we need to plan the beam spread of light to cover the entire area that the sculpture will move through. At left, one sculpture moves side to side while pieces of the other move in circles.

Gathering Tools and Techniques **Learning to Paint with Light**
SECTION I

Sculpting Elements – Water

Water and electricity don't mix. This requires the equipment to be sturdy and solidly water-proof. We have to think about where the cables and other accessory equipment get placed to hide them from view. Limitations can effect the lighting. At left, the stone lion has some light on its face from pedestal mount underwater fixtures. The amount of light varies on the growth of the plantings, which will require attention and pruning over time.

In this little feature, two of these fixtures provide light for the lion as well as light on the sprays as well as showing the goose in silhouette.

I prefer to keep lighting equipment out of the water whenever it makes sense. That will always be less dramatic.

In this Ohio backyard, landscape architect Emery Rogers planned a series of spouts and falls starting in the pool to the left of the summer house and continuing throughout the building. At right, you can see that the fixtures recessed into the bottom of the floor, light the water fall and spill onto the interesting texture of the stone wall. Near the edge of the building a smooth-edged waterfall has lighting located in front of the fall to shine on the smooth surface of falling water with no air bubbles. This condition requires light to shine directly at that falling water from in front in order to reflect a sheen of light in order for any light effect to be seen. This is otherwise considered glare, so we have to plan the aiming angle so it doesn't shine directly into viewer's eyes.

Inside the building the runnel can be a seat. At the end, there are fixtures recessed into the pool floor. Here, the weir, where the water begins to fall, is rough creating air bubbles in the water that catches light, making the waterfall glow.

Learning to Paint with Light *Gathering Tools and Techniques*
SECTION I
Creating an Outdoor Room

Gathering Tools and Techniques **Learning to Paint with Light**
SECTION I

Creating an Outdoor Room

Extending personal space includes creating outdoor rooms. In warm areas, this can be a year round usable space. In areas with cold seasons, lighting outside spaces provides a view reconnecting us with our garden spaces. One early outdoor room I worked on is the Chardonnay Garden entertainment room at Far Niente in the Napa Valley. In the image, lower left, I met with Gil Nickel in January in the pouring rain to discuss this portion of the landscape lighting. With landscape architect Jonathan Plant (jonathanplant.com) designing, the space was developing during construction - which had to be done by June for Gil's wedding to Beth. We had only an overall site plan (p.28) showing gardens to be developed. I blew up that plan, numbered trees and elements, and marked up photos of those trees and elements using a Polaroid camera, so that I could hand it to the contractor in the field as the lighting developed.

This space is used for lunches, dinners, and events. Mature Quercus suber/Cork Oaks were planted long ago and now shade the new food and wine bars. Approaching from across the bridge, we used a warmer light on the stone under the counters to attract arriving guests attention to help them know where to go for food and wine. Using the Cork Oaks and the Live Oaks for downlighting, we lit the bridge over the pond getting guests back and forth from the pavilion to the dining tables set up on the lawn.

I used downlight in the trees to light the counters. We lit the counters to a brighter level, again helping attract guests and show them what was on the menu, or which wines were being served that night.

In the upper left photo you see the dance floor area. It can be used for many differing purposes, so the lighting extends over the entire area. We placed fixtures to shine down through branches creating patterns across the dance floor.

Learning to Paint with Light *Gathering Tools and Techniques*
SECTION I
Creating an Outdoor Room

Just outside the kitchen at this Northern California home, the patio has lounge chairs and a dining table. Looking from the table to the other end of the space, you can see a sculpture that serves as the focal point for that viewing direction. Lush planting on all sides of that space provides vertical elements to light at night to create this outdoor room's 'walls'.

Because there is a large grade change, the garden designer, Valerie Matzge,r included the trellis and the curved set of stairs. She used moss as the edge of the tread up against the step's riser. This provides a good contrast for us to help identify the steps after dark.

A Jacaranda mimosifolia tree (not seen) has numerous downlights to light the table and surrounding planting areas.

Gathering Tools and Techniques **Learning to Paint with Light**
SECTION I

Creating an Outdoor Room

The lighting is a combination of up and downlighting with stake mount, below grade, eave mount, and tree mounted fixtures. Placement was carefully planned to accentuate the characteristics of the plants, provide task lighting for meals, and safety lighting identifying curbs and grade changes. All through an aesthetic approach, which can be done for most if not all night lighting situations.

At the trellis, notice the brightness on the horizontal beam. I did not use the black paint inside the glare shields, as I wanted to make sure guests, after a glass of wine, knew that the stairs existed. Notice that the light level at the top of the stairs is higher than other ground areas – again, as a way to introduce the stairs.

The lighting levels vary throughout the scene, creating a rich space to enjoy at the end of a hard day.

Learning to Paint with Light *Gathering Tools and Techniques*
SECTION I
Creating an Outdoor Room

Below, the sculpture's extended arm has a bird landing for a drink, and it points the way to the garden's exit. From the lower remote seating area it also provides a signal for getting back to the house. This garden extension wraps around an area originally part of this property, but sold off many years ago. Lighting continues the lit wall effect surrounding the walkway and stairs linking all the spaces. Just beyond the man, tall trees allow for downlighting, so the technique varies, but the overall appearance continues.

The stairs here are not lit as brightly as the previous page's. Rather, a soft downlight shows both tread and riser, with two pathlights along the lower edges. Look at the new landscape space done in 2019 in Section III, p189.

Gathering Tools and Techniques **Learning to Paint with Light**
SECTION I

Creating an Outdoor Room

At the remote colonnade, the furniture changes from time to time with chairs sometimes and dining tables others. Surface-mount adjustable downlights attached to the trellis structure allow for various purposes over time. Below, some of the lighting softly grazes the hedge and some downlights the seating area. Adjustable stake mount uplights wash the columns and spills up onto the vines covering the trellis.

Learning to Paint with Light *Gathering Tools and Techniques*
SECTION I
Understanding People Moving Though Space – Physical and Visual

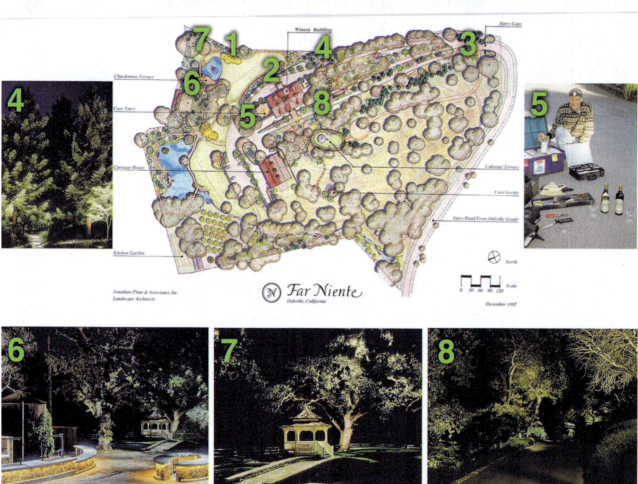

This Far Niente site map illustrates the movement lighting we need to provide after dark. When invited to an event, you get dropped at the Redwood Walk, see the photo and location on the site plan (#4). From there you cross the lawn passing the Main Winery Building (#2), on your left, as you travel toward the lake, passing the Birch Grove (#1) on your right. Dining tables get set up by the gazebo (#7) and you cross the bridge over to the food and wine counters (#6) and then back to sit and relax.

When you leave at the end of the evening, your car uses the exit road (#8) to reach the gates (#3) then continuing along the drive to reach the road. All landscape lighting requires maintenance to keep the lighting scenes functioning as they should. Photo #5 shows Michael Hooker on site with all the tools and supplies we bring, with the addition of some wine, thanks to the owner Gil Nickel.

Gathering Tools and Techniques **Learning to Paint with Light**
SECTION I
How Light Welcomes Guests

The entry needs to be clear when arriving at a home or business. In the upper photo, in the Berkeley Hills, an existing post fixture provides some general lighting. I added downlighting for the door and along the vine over the wall with some plant lighting surrounding the walk. All this softens the brightness of that existing fixture.

In Marin, the front door is not visible from the drive. I lit trees on the left, along with the stairs and brought the light level up at the covered patio by the front door. Lighting clues like these help people understand a space. In this case, we added new sconces at the garage and the interior lighting of the family room lanai. Those three elements with similar brightness reinforce the idea of finding the stairs to arrive at the entry.

This kind of gentle guidance helps people find their destination and says to them that they are welcome.

Learning to Paint with Light *Gathering Tools and Techniques*
SECTION I
How Light Welcomes Guests

Providing the brightest amount of light at the door signals the destination. It can be quite simple, even when the door is not. Here, two adjustable low voltage downlights have narrow beams with a linear spread lens. The lens causes the light to become a narrow streak of light. Here I cross-aim them to light the bronze art panels on this door and two others at the site.

While this may look like a lot of light – it isn't really. Light walls surrounding the door increases the sense of brightness due to light reflecting off them. This was done long before LED sources were available for architectural use, but at that time it only took two 20-watt lamps. With LED we could reduce that to between 2 – 4 watts each!

Gathering Tools and Techniques **Learning to Paint with Light**
SECTION I

Seeing the Importance of Shadows

Michael Hooker, my design partner of many years used to say 'Darkness is your friend'. One of the things he meant is that varying light levels show details and texture. You can create patterns on a wall, as I did here in the SF Showhouse above, using what I called 'anti-shadows'. Normally, when you light a cactus as I have here, the effect on the wall would be a dark pattern of the plant. This visual enhanced the playful nature of this attic retreat, designed by Karen Kitowski, (karenkitowski.com).

At the hallway one the right, you walk through after entering the SF Garden Show space called the 'Garden of Dreams', on your way to a series of other imaginary spaces. The team created 'cloud walls' by crunching up architectural vellum paper and stacking them to make walls and ceilings. Michael then lit them from multiple angles, front and back, and used sky blue color to create the appearance of the walls being clouds.

Their otherworldliness included that door to nowhere painting, with the actual doorway being lit slightly brighter on the right to help you find your way onward.

Design Intuition Takes Over: Honing the Art
Refining and Expanding Design Techniques

Time is a good teacher. In landscape lighting this means spending a lot of time in gardens at night, seeing how light can sculpt a space. Dramatic effects work in public spaces, especially theme parks, but, for many public and residential spaces, softer lighting aids relaxing and recovering from a stressful day or week!

The space above, in Ohio, has only downlighting. I like to start with downlighting, as it appears natural, and gives us multiple benefits – it can cover more territory; it is out of harm's way so the effects last longer, and the fixtures don't get damaged or knocked around by gardeners and animals. You can see that the lighting isn't 'even' as I used more candlepower and a narrower beam spread in some areas, or less output with wider beam spreads in other areas.

Over the years, I learned that softer light actually works better in most spaces. Our brain/eye system works amazingly well in low light levels and softer light acts like a gentle reminder to unwind and take it easy for a few minutes. Walking through a lit garden gives you time to contemplate.

The area surrounding the central grouping of trees and shrubs is lit more completely as the focal area of this scene, I placed grazing light on trunks and parts of canopies making the framework for this view from the path. Views help guide people as they traverse through multiple experiences before returning home or to the party. I left the background completely dark – encouraging visitors to keep exploring along the path.

Design Intuition Takes Over: Honing the Art
SECTION II

Refining and Expanding Design Techniques

This allée in Villanova, Pennsylvania frames the view to this home. I lit the trunks on the 'inside' of the space, leaving trunks and canopies dark on the outside, due to neighbors on all sides of this space. Each tree has a pair of stake mount uplights; one for the trunk and one aimed at the center of the canopy, creating this ethereal space on your way to visit.

Design Intuition Takes Over: Honing the Art
SECTION II
Visual Composition

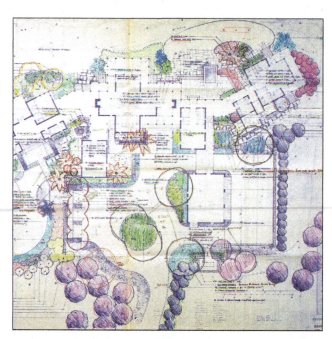

Sometimes we start planning lighting before the landscape exists, We need to think about all the elements in the space. Deciding how we will create the night view starts here and ends with aiming. As much design is done during aiming, as any other time in the project. I used tree mount lights in the island trees to downlight the ground plane and reveal the edges of the circle. Additional downlights graze the wall to the left of the entry stairs, the edge of the drive under the tree on the right, between the circle and the stairs, and in the overhang above the stairs guiding your eyes to the dark front door. I convinced the artist/owner to put light-colored objects on the stairs to help people find the entry.

Design Intuition Takes Over: Honing the Art
SECTION II
Visual Composition

To the left of that entry circle is the guest entry gate. Between the trees are parking spaces and the entry arbor is lit to identify the guest entry (left side of plan). Notice that I always make sure that you can see the latch to open the gate without having to fumble.

Then, the scene continues inside the gate and culminates at the far bed with downlighting on newly planted trees and shrubs. That planting will grow up to fill in the scene over the years. Identifying the boundary allows guests unfamiliar with the space to not have to think about the space, and easily move toward the guest wing entrance – which is at an angle to the right after you go through the entry arbor.

On the landscape plan for this South Carolina property, I colored elements to help me understand the landscape designer's vision. Spending this time helps me build a view of the space in my mind's eye and allows me time to think about how the space will look when first completed, and how it will change over the seasons and through the course of years. I prepare my projects for future growth and change from the beginning.

Design Intuition Takes Over: Honing the Art
SECTION II
Visual Composition

Lighting trees behind the house, even very softly, helps complete the shape of the building. In the front, tree uplight spills onto the white roof edge also contributing to showing the shape. Understanding how light can have double purpose allows us to build a scene without actually lighting everything.

Design Intuition Takes Over: Honing the Art
SECTION II
Visual Composition

In Upstate New York most outdoor night activity happens during the time trees have their leaves. I have lit the kitchen porch to a higher level for outdoor meals, games, whatever the family and guests want to do. Having that brighter outdoor level next to the more brightly lit kitchen space aids your eye/brain transition as you leave the brighter space and spill out into softer landscape lighting levels.

Downlighting reveals the patio space, the top of the seat wall, and of course, the dog sculpture (Handsome Dan of Yale fame!). Showing ground plane elements adds to our sense of comfort in a darkish space.

Design Intuition Takes Over: Honing the Art
SECTION II
Visual Composition

The walkway you see in these two photos provides an illusion of access to this front door. The actual walk from the driveway intersects this path on the other side of that raised stone wall (refer to the upper left in drawing), because the house is set at an angle on the property. The lower left photo, next page, shows the view as you enter the property. Lighting trees along the drive helps the owner and guests approach the parking area, at which point you can then continue left along the path to the entry courtyard. For gatherings, the pergola on the right side of the drive beckons you to move in that direction. All along the walk, plants are lit to help guide guests to the back of this Ohio property.

Design Intuition Takes Over: Honing the Art
SECTION II

Visual Composition

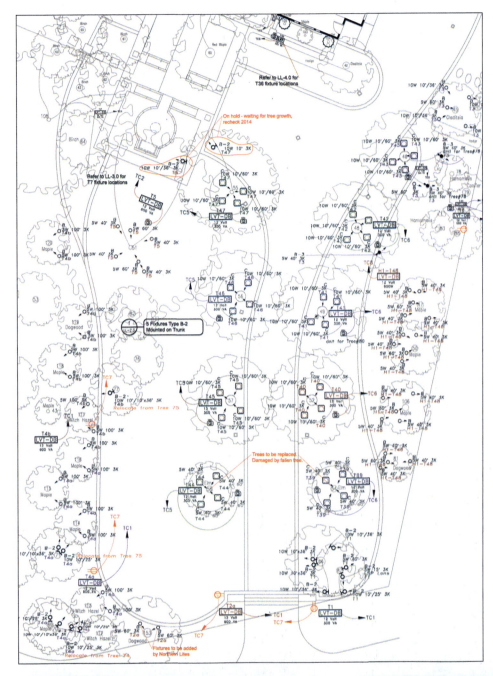

Thinking about how someone will navigate a complicated site, especially when they are unfamiliar, can help them enjoy the space by lighting elements providing visual clues along the way as they move towards their destination.

A secondary walk from the parking area allows guests to walk directly to the back entertainment space without going through the house. Lighting trees, hedges, walls along the drive, and that walk will provide visual comfort. Downlighting at the pergola then shows the way around the house to the back patio and gardens.

All these visual aids need to coalesce, working together to create a beautiful rendition of the landscape after dark. Providing a stable composition can accommodate safety and security and give the owner a wonderful night space to enjoy.

Design Intuition Takes Over: Honing the Art
SECTION II

Visual Composition

Looking back along the driveway toward the street, lighting on both sides of the property shows the expanse of the space, and in the fall gives a wonderful experience of the trees changing color.

Throughout a woodland edge like this, the lighting level among trees can vary. I will typically light smaller specimen trees along the edge to a brighter level than the driveway trees, helping to bring your eye back to the ground.

Varying the light level makes the scene more visually interesting. I always want to make sure I bring the viewer's eyes back to human scale, so I will typically light larger trees more softly than smaller trees, allowing your eye to come back to the ground. The large deciduous tree that is brighter in the photo above is at the end of the entry walk configuration (from the front door view, see drawing on page 39), so I increased its light level bringing your eye to the end of that view from the front door. Note that some of the large trees in that front lawn are not lit at all, crafting a view that has continuity and will make sense for people unfamiliar with the site. Some of those unlit trees do hold downlights for that border edge.

Design Intuition Takes Over: Honing the Art
SECTION II
View Out a Window

I am finishing this book during the Covid-19 pandemic. We have all spent significantly more time in our homes and our property than perhaps prior to this outbreak. One of the benefits landscape lighting gives us is making our interior spaces feel larger when anything is lit out the window. Lighting the landscape outside our windows reconnects us with our outdoor space, as well. Here in Northern California, you'd think the owners would be outside often but the San Francisco Bay Area cools off most evenings.

In Upstate New York, having a view from the kitchen window of a distant apple tree connects us to the garden in summer and winter when it's way too cold to spend much time outside, even when the ground isn't covered with several feet of snow. The daytime photo shows that you can provide a view into the garden even when the object tree is a long way from the window.

Design Intuition Takes Over: Honing the Art
SECTION II
View Out a Window

View can change due to your position adjacent to the window. Sitting on this window seat in Upstate New York, you are closer to the view than when you stand beside the seat. The view also changes from one season to another and from day to night. Having a view at night, whether seated or standing, enhances the room and can make the space feel larger. When someone is seated, we need to make sure they won't see any glare from the uplights lighting those trees just outside the window. Avoiding glare always comes back to fixture position, aiming, and shielding.

Design Intuition Takes Over: Honing the Art
SECTION II

Planning Movement Through Space

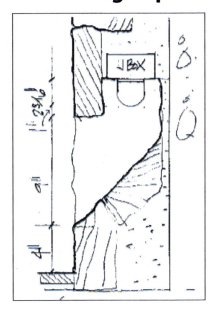

Some properties, like this one in Napa Valley, CA, are expansive. This upper photo shows the arrival circle as you continue up a long driveway hill. We recessed fixtures into the driveway circle wall to make sure that you see that the drive ends. Notice that even with the light source hidden from view, the effect of light on the stone is much stronger than the surrounding light. In this case, having that visual clue helps, but often that much light level variation is too strong, distracting from the landscape itself.

In the distance, beyond that drive circle, are vineyards which remain unlit. Up the hill and a great distance away is the tennis court area. Lighting the trees surrounding the courts provides a distant view from the main house location. On the next page, you can see the distance between the two areas. In both photos, the tree grouping doesn't seem as far away as it actually is, due to leaving the vineyards dark. That darkness shortens the sense of depth perception.

Design Intuition Takes Over: Honing the Art
SECTION II
Planning Movement Through Space

This family Napa Valley residential estate compound has multiple building and garden spaces. Providing a sense of cohesion while allowing each to stand alone visually is critical – not just for large spaces but for all landscapes. Using similar techniques, balanced brightness levels, and visual cues helps provide cohesion. I prefer to use downlighting for pathways, especially in scenarios like this one, but it isn't always possible.

Design Intuition Takes Over: Honing the Art
SECTION II

Planning Movement Through Space

The circulation through this landscape is complex. You arrive at the circle up a long winding drive that goes up a hill. Along the way are gates. Uplighting clusters of evergreen trees provides a visual cue that a change is coming.

Notice that I did not provide lighting along the drive outside the gate on the way to the main house. Automobiles have headlights. The night lighting is more for pedestrian traffic and providing the visual clues for movement through the property.

The main tree in the lower courtyard is this palm tree lit with uplights in its planter. Its trunk brightness matches that of the entrance to the wine cellar, but is still softer than the sconce over the stairs through a tunnel up to the Main House, and the sconces along the walk up left at the second residence, announcing those buildings and entries.

Look at the difference of light level on the two stair walls from the courtyard to the 2nd Residence. Reflected light off the walk from the wall-recessed fixtures provides a very low wash on the further wall, visually separating the two in this normal lighting scene.

For parties, the strings of lights are strung from the multi-level garage upper wall across to the stair wall. This doesn't add any 'task' lighting but creates a party mood. While brighter than the lighting of the big Oak trees around the courtyard, it is the contrast of color from the much warmer lamps in the string lights to the cooler color of the foliage, along with the sparkle, that adds a festive feel.

Design Intuition Takes Over: Honing the Art
SECTION II

Planning Movement Through Space

This 300+ acre site in Ohio requires thought for both movement along all the pedestrian pathways and views from one area to another. In the middle of the photo is the main house – not the house at the top of the photo, the security building. Just below and to the right of the main house are multiple structures – the pool house, overlook, Birch Alley Gate structure, outdoor chapel and the boathouse.

From autumn above to spring below, the view across the lake from the boathouse changes due to the lack of leaves once the trees go dormant during the cold months. We lit some of the existing big trees and some of the new evergreen trees.

The big issue that this scene challenges us to consider is change over the years. Not just the growth of the evergreen trees and how that will impact the scene, but the growth of the multiple 'newly' planted deciduous trees that will also have an impact. We planned power and transformer locations for additional fixtures to be added over time.

Design Intuition Takes Over: Honing the Art
SECTION II

Planning Movement Through Space

Design Intuition Takes Over: Honing the Art
SECTION II
Planning Movement Through Space

At each of the structures surrounding the main house, downlights within and around the buildings, in addition to the landscape lighting, provides usable light on and inside each building. Several locations required completely shielded wall and path lights to continue the walk lighting, so as not interfere with the scene.

Design Intuition Takes Over: Honing the Art
SECTION II
Visual Destination

Some landscape spaces are not meant to be used or even made for people to be in them. On the right side of a house this oval patio space provides a view along a circular walk to the front entry for a home in Northern CA. Viewed from the street, from the living room, and as you walk to the front door, it completes the front scene of this house with another folly-like garden on the left side of the house. Often we think of one object as the view but it can be entire garden spaces.

Design Intuition Takes Over: Honing the Art
SECTION II
Visual Destination

More typically, one feature will be lit brighter than the surrounding plantings – here, a tree. It could be a sculpture or a water feature that provides a view or a visual destination. The use of this brighter element to resolve a view can be used for more than one purpose. Here, the idea is to invite you to continue walking through this Upstate NY garden. Essentially a contemplation garden, the owners walked it whenever they could return from Japan, and always with guests.

Notice that I try, whenever possible, to install no path lighting. Not only do I mean there are no path lights, which can distract from the garden day or night, but there are no lights whose purpose is to light the path. My go-to technique is to light things around the path. Here, downlighting from a large, mature tree along the street side of the garden reveals the hedge, the wall, the plantings on the street side of the wall, and the water trough.

The path is clearly and comfortably lit for the owners and guests to meander through the garden. When I plan the beam spread and then aim the lights, I make sure that there is enough spill light, which will be much softer than the main candlepower in the central portion of even an LED, to provide very low level light on the path. When a path is surrounded by lit elements, especially vertical elements, not much lighting on the path is required for safe and comfortable movement, even when the path is uneven. Our brain/eye system can accommodate so well that obstacles can be seen in very low light levels.

Design Intuition Takes Over: Honing the Art
SECTION II

Visual Destination

Wandering through a property in Montgomery County, PA, this stream is an important view from multiple locations – from several places in the main house, the pool garden, bridges, and walkways that criss cross the stream as it makes its way down hill. We selected multiple trees along the length of the stream and downlit the falls and the rocks that frame the waterway. Glimpses connect the stream from the top of the property all the way down past the back of the main house. This lighting is on its own control load so that if the owners want to see only the stream, they can.

Depending on the location, varying degrees of downlighting is incorporated. In some areas, a few trees have soft uplighting and the ground cover surrounding a group of trees will be downlit to a very low level, filling out the scene.

The patio in the upper photo on page 100 is one of the multiple viewing locations. You can look as well to the pool or back to the house from the pool.

Design Intuition Takes Over: Honing the Art
SECTION II
Visual Destination

Landscape lighting is always softer than interior lighting, so it's easy to see to and into the interior rooms. Framing this view to the house, trees selected on the left and right have light level variation in the canopy with the higher level getting close to the light level of the interior space. Using both up and downlighting, the trees are filled out with softer light so that the entire tree doesn't have to be as bright as the light inside the window.

Design Intuition Takes Over: Honing the Art
SECTION II

Visual Destination

It isn't often that the lighting designer is included in major decisions about the landscape design itself. For this Pennsylvania project, originally developed well over 150 years ago, the hedge in the back yard became a big issue. Carpinus betulus/Hornbeam has been used as hedging for centuries. This one was in the middle of the back of the property and a very large tree at the edge of the property could be seen above the hedge. The question was whether to cut a viewing space out of the hedge to allow the entire tree to be seen and all the way to the back.

In the photos above you can see the hedge before the cut, as well as big mature trees nearby the hedge. I used those trees to downlight the hedge, so that at night you could still see the undulation of the hedge – or maybe even see that shape better than during the day. Downlights carefully placed in the overhanging branches of the trees provided the exact placement to graze the hedge and create brightness variation that enhanced the shape of the hedge.

The above photos show the view from the kitchen, living area, and dining room – an important view.

Design Intuition Takes Over: Honing the Art
SECTION II

Visual Destination

When first done in the early 2000s, a bench had been ordered but not yet delivered when this photo was taken. Obviously, this was before LED, so the color of the red fall leaves on the hedge shows warm. With two young trees planted at the base of the large, mature tree, no additional lighting was required for that tall tree.

Design Intuition Takes Over: Honing the Art
SECTION II

Sculpting Elements – Trees and Plants

At the Chicago Botanic Gardens, this Fagus/Beech tree is the donor tree. The upper right photo shows the mockup my team did for the Board of Directors, along with other parts of the gardens on Evening Island, for approval to continue with our design. The lower photo shows the final lighting, requiring multiple fixtures under the branching and multiple outside the canopy to show the tree's overall form.

Design Intuition Takes Over: Honing the Art
SECTION II
Sculpting Elements – Trees and Plants

Some big trees, even when mature, don't have stunning form without their leaves in the winter. Yet, when those same trees are lit, they look as beautiful as any other season, maybe better. Even though trees are tall, you don't need a spot light or a lot of candlepower to light them. What you do need is enough fixtures around them to show their structural form, the full canopy, and at least one fixture visually tying the trunk to the ground, either up or down.

Design Intuition Takes Over: Honing the Art
SECTION II

Sculpting Elements – Trees and Plants

Some trees are either pruned or grow in a lopsided shape, as the one above in Ohio. On this tree, plants on the right side limited the tree's right canopy. As we were planning the fixture layout along this entry road at a crucial turn in the road, we needed this tree. To make it not look lopsided, I had to light multiple trees around it on that side.

The evergreens at right are Ilex/Hollies. This genus has very dense leaves and most species have a very dense leaf overlap making the entire canopy dense from the ground to the tip. To light them, I placed fixtures outside the canopy at a grazing angle to show their incredible texture. Notice on the right tree you can see some branching structure. This is not something you can count on with Hollies. Like many evergreen and coniferous trees, lighting them gently is difficult due to the dense canopy, shiny top leaf finish, and branching to the ground habit.

On the next page is the conceptual description I submitted to the client from my office in New York for this portion of this Northern CA property. A front and back view of the lighting is on the top.

Design Intuition Takes Over: Honing the Art
SECTION II
Sculpting Elements – Trees and Plants

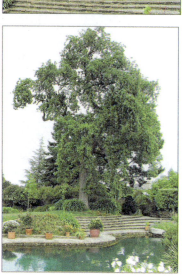

Pool Area

Oak # 2 will be lit as part of the 'West View'. In addition, Type SA-1 and/or SB-1 downlights will softly light the planting areas around walkways and stairs. This fixture quantity will be based on how much of the area isn't covered by the 'West View' fixtures. There might be some locations that we want to 'double' up using path light fixtures for a very quiet scene.

Existing path fixtures that should remain will be replaced with a shrouded fixture to be selected. There are approximately 25 throughout the property. This quantity needs to be determined. Additional path light fixture locations need to be identified.

Trees #4 and 5 are uplit as part of the 'West View'.

We had discussed maybe having one or two outdoor 'torchères'. We will review that option and determine if any other general lighting is needed in the pool area.

Design Intuition Takes Over: Honing the Art
SECTION II
Sculpting Elements – Trees and Plants

This view across an Ohio property lake serves as a great teaching scene. All the big trees are deciduous; part of the farm field border from many years ago. As this landscape developed as a homestead in the 2000s, additional trees were added, but the mature trees remain. I discussed with the team how much of that view across the new lake, from the boat house, we should light. The owners didn't limit us, but I decided that we should limit the view to the group in the middle of this photo. As we started lighting them I knew I wanted both up and downlighting, as there is a walking path in front of the trees and a lot of ground plane specimen trees, shrubs, and ground cover being added.

I decided to put the uplights on one control zone and the downlights on another. That allowed for looking at the tree group three ways: uplights only, downlights only, and the combination of up and down lighting (see next page). This was a big site with extensive landscape lighting, so, the one decision we limited ourselves to was no dimming. We had to get the light level balance right without dimming.

On next page, the top photo includes both up and downlighting, showing both ground plane and the tree canopies. In the lower left photo you see uplighting only. It is ok, but without the ground plane, doesn't provide as complete a scene and makes the space less visually comfortable.

Then, the lower right shows downlighting only. This confirms my tenet that you cannot only downlight. The top of the canopy is gone, there are hot spots on trunks and branches, and it just doesn't look good. When doing big trees, a combination of up and downlighting works best. It looks the most complete, and those hot spots that are needed for some downlighting locations blend in and are not objectionable.

Design Intuition Takes Over: Honing the Art
SECTION II

Sculpting Elements – Trees and Plants

Design Intuition Takes Over: Honing the Art
SECTION II

Sculpting Elements – Trees and Plants

Understanding how two tree elements will look together in different seasons is important: Here, we are seeing winter on the left and summer on the right.

A group of young trees in spring and fall.

A forest scene that has been augmented with newer plantings by the owners, as seen in winter and summer.

Design Intuition Takes Over: Honing the Art
SECTION II
Sculpting Elements – Trees and Plants

As shown in the upper pair of photos, some young trees have interesting form even in winter, while others take time to develop their form. Notice in the upper right that the tall, mature trees are lit from the lighting of the new young trees so don't need their own fixtures. That soft light adds a lot to the scene.

Above you see another Hornbeam hedge, pruned to reveal the decorative wall beneath the canopy and also as a screen to create privacy from an adjacent golf course. Dense canopies don't easily light through to the top. This changes from summer, the in-leaf season, to fall when the leaves start to become more translucent.

To show the wall detail and create a luminous effect in the hedge, I used one fixture in between each trunk to get some light on the trunk, the wall, and up into the canopy. In the middle photo you can see the relationship to a tree trunk; the fixture positioning set to straight up to get maximum light distribution on the three elements; and setting the glare shield to avoid seeing the lit inside of the fixture housing from the summer house.

Design Intuition Takes Over: Honing the Art
SECTION II

Sculpting Elements – Trees and Plants

These three images are the same tree at a Long Island, NY property. It is a very large Oak that you can see from the pool area and from the rear porches. Because it's so tall, you can see the canopy over the garage roof from the front and from multiple angles, including the walk down to the Peconic Bay. I lit the trunk and branching structure for all views.

Big trees like this one require multiple fixtures to light the entire tree. A total of 20 stake mount uplights which varied from 25° beam spread to one at 60° beam spread under that low branch! No tight beams were needed, which is typical. We also had six tree-mount downlights, placed in nearby pairs down lighting the grass, rocks, and the pathway to the dock area (you can see the path lighting' brightness behind the tree below left).

Using multiple fixtures allows you to show the three-dimensional form, including the branching structure. In both views of the lit tree, above, you can see shadows at the top of the canopy where it remains dark. Variation of brightness throughout the canopy adds interest to the trees overall appearance. A tree like this one is easily 80 – 100'/24 –30 meters wide and in the range of 50 – 80'/15 – 25 meters high.

Tree downlighting requires working with an arborist. I like to consult with the arborist on the tree's health before planning to mount fixtures in the tree. Once given the go-ahead, we need to plan installation sessions with the safety of the arborists as our top priority. They throw ropes to provide them a solid connection in case anything goes wrong so that they stay connected to a part of the tree and have a safe path down to the ground. Watching them move through the trees is an amazing site. They need to be provided with supplies like head-lamps, cordless drills, eyelet cable ties, appropriate screws, etc. And the fixtures have to be prewired before sending them up the tree. With the arborist in the tree, we try to pre-aim the fixtures and set the glare shields during daylight installation. Using that approach on this site, we were able to reduce the need for them to go back up into trees by 60%.

Design Intuition Takes Over: Honing the Art
SECTION II
Sculpting Elements – Trees and Plants

For tree-mount fixtures, ladders, and ropes get set during the day and left for night-aiming.

The process goes more quickly when the property can accommodate articulating lift trucks. You can see how intertwined the bucket is inside this canopy, which requires the operator to have patience and skill, especially after dark.

These trees are on Long Island, St. Paul, MN., and St. Helena, CA.

Design Intuition Takes Over: Honing the Art
SECTION II

Sculpting Elements – Trees and Plants

Palms and tree ferns have fronds instead of branches with leaves and can be quite large and heavy. Lighting for a palm is typically uplighting, as they grow so tall. In all four images, the canopies are unevenly lit, with shadowing. Tree ferns vary by genus and species in height ranging from 3'/1 meter to 30'/10 meters. Some remain low enough to downlight from an adjacent taller tree or a building.

The palm in the lower left photo is a good example of a time to break the basic rule of a minimum of three fixtures per tree to reveal three dimensional form. With that palm being up against a light colored wall, we used two fixtures aimed slightly toward the wall, creating shadows and reflecting enough light onto the back of the canopy.

Design Intuition Takes Over: Honing the Art
SECTION II
Sculpting Elements – Paths, Walkways, and Stairs

While lighting water is the most difficult lighting task to tackle, stairs and pathways are perhaps the most misunderstood and often treated too cavalierly. Throwing a bunch of unshielded path lights along this stairway would disrupt the serene experience. This apple tree, lit as part of ILLI's training permanent installation (See page 304), has only three stake-mount uplights for the tree itself and five ring-mount downlights, one over the grass and one over the ground cover near the base of the stairs. The two lighting the stairs are 3W, 50°, 3K, and finally the one lighting the base of the stairs is located higher in the tree.

My basic philosophy for paths and stairs is to light planting or other objects on one or both sides of the walk and let light spill over onto the path. That means the path will typically be lit more softly, allowing people to enjoy the garden elements. Without fixtures over people's heads, no disrupting shadows make the walk uncomfortable and you can clearly see the uneven steps here.

Design Intuition Takes Over: Honing the Art
SECTION II

Sculpting Elements – Paths, Walkways, and Stairs

This path with stairs from the driveway to the kitchen door in Upstate NY, at the ILLI permanent installation (See page 312) is a good example of difficult paths/stairs. Originally installed in the 1920s and modified over time, the stairs remain uneven and nonstandard in layout. For safety reasons, attention needs to be called to this awkward stair layout. Early on, using ring-mount fixtures in the Magnolia trees flanking the walk (photo lower right), I provided high contrast at step locations. Once additional lighting was added for the kitchen garden, the ILLI team softened that contrast (photo at top), but it still has light level variation so that you see the change in elevation.

Design Intuition Takes Over: Honing the Art
SECTION II

Sculpting Elements – Paths, Walkways, and Stairs

At this arrival court in Napa, these stairs lead to a remote parking area, and while it needed lighting, we didn't want this staircase to distract from the main entry. Using ring-mount fixtures, located in the left tree, the stairs are clearly lit and still softer than the lighting of the large pot.

In Upstate NY on a wooded site, these stairs have one fixture mounted on the building eaves to introduce these remote stairs, but not draw attention to them.

Design Intuition Takes Over: Honing the Art
SECTION II

Sculpting Elements – Paths, Walkways, and Stairs

These two stairs on a project in Northern CA are at a remote location (top) and the main patio (lower). Landscape designer Valerie Matzger designed them to reference each other in shape. At the main patio she used moss on each level between the riser and the stair tread, above. I lit the stairs evenly and to a high light level for safety using fixtures attached to the structure on both sides. As an entertainment patio where wine is served, I felt I needed to grab guests' attention to notice the stairs while they chatted with other guests and wandered away from the patio. At the remote stairs (top), downlights mounted in the Redwood trees very softly wash the lower stairs, with brighter light on the mid landing and upper stairs leading back to the sculpture. I added to copper path lights at the lower, back edges, as a visual cue for guests at that lower level.

Design Intuition Takes Over: Honing the Art
SECTION II
Sculpting Elements – Paths, Walkways, and Stairs

At the Rain Wall garden on Long Island, NY, down a set of stairs from the pool patio and just outside the exercise room, the stair lighting is much quieter. Used primarily by the owners, we needed to make sure that a person can navigate the stairs, without detracting from the rain wall as people descended. Using a similar concept to that I showed you in that Napa arrival circle (p43), I modified an LED fixture to be recessed into the stone wall.

The shape of the opening in the stone was restricted by what the stone masons felt comfortable carving. Note the quick disconnect connection, with enough cable to pull the fixture out if any maintenance was required. It being an early LED installation for these fixtures and all the rain wall fixtures, I specified ordering a full set of replacements stored on site, just in case.

I'll talk more about the rain wall on pages 123-128, but this photo shows the space between the structural wall behind the rain wall and the rain wall itself. A matter of only six inches required careful thought as to how to accomplish that lighting.

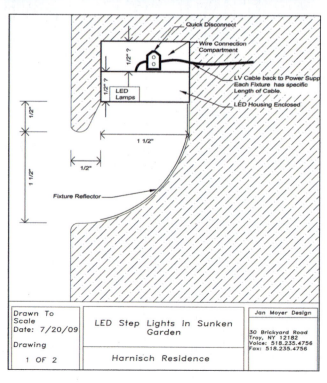

Design Intuition Takes Over: Honing the Art
SECTION II

Sculpting Elements – Paths, Walkways, and Stairs

On the same project, this sunken walk is completely hidden from view on the site. At the stairs and in the rock walls, we used miniature MR8 LEDs made for this project early on in LED use in landscape lighting. These have tiny stakes so we tucked them in crevices here and at other stone walls in the front.

Along the walk itself, tree mount fixtures wash the walls and spill onto the path. Some trees were selected for lighting, like the one at the end of the photo or very background tree, at right.

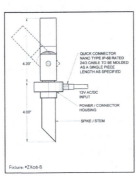

Design Intuition Takes Over: Honing the Art
SECTION II
Sculpting Elements – Paths, Walkways, and Stairs

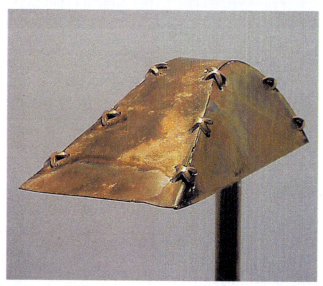

Over the years, many projects have called for custom fixtures to represent that project. For the Chicago Botanic Garden (CBG), Mike Hartman, Escort Lighting (escortlighting.com), and I designed this copper fixture for the Evening Island lighting project. We designed other compatible fixtures for other garden spaces, (see page 89).

This one was used all along the walk at the back of Evening Island, (top photos), as well as other areas on the island. The planting material varied along the walk, including the height and height variation throughout the summer growing season. In many areas, the perennials disappeared completely at the end of the season until the next spring. These varying conditions required careful thought as to what would work best in all situations.

The final design includes a scooped form on the back with slight splaying on both the sides, and a long widening angle for the front. This provides as much distribution, in all directions, as possible, and completely shields the lamp from view in all cases.

We added the 'stitching' detail as a design element identifying it as a CBG fixture. In the upper photos, you can see that pools of light are created even with very wide light throw. We needed to spread out the spacing as far as possible but still provide a sense of safe passage on this remote path. As I typically do, I placed the fixtures all on one side to avoid a spotty appearance. This also reduces wiring and installation costs.

Design Intuition Takes Over: Honing the Art
SECTION II

Sculpting Elements – Paths, Walkways, and Stairs

At this site in Montgomery County, PA, a series of paths allow the owners and guests to enjoy this expansive wooded property. At top, the Cornus kousa/Kousa Dogwood has four ring-mount fixtures to downlight the ground cover and spill over onto the walkway, providing soft even light as you navigate this tight space. This corner is behind the house, just beyond the back patio, and is one of the views from the back patio. It is reached along the path of the lower left photo and continues along the lower right path to the pool, pool house, and pool patio. The brickwork, at lower left, is interesting and shows clearly.

At the lower right path to the pool area, lights in trees above additional Kousa Dogwoods create the patterns on the walk. Those trees and the ones in the lower left photo have uplighting as well. At the end of the lower right path is a stately Acer palmatum/Japanese Maple more brightly lit as a visual destination and focal point at the pool garden space.

Along the left side of the corner we used a series of path lights between the garden space, lower left and the corner. At both of the spaces shown in the lower photos, we used downlights mounted in large, mature trees, visible in the upper left daytime photo, to provide the garden fill light with spill onto the paths.

Design Intuition Takes Over: Honing the Art
SECTION II
Sculpting Elements – Paths, Walkways, and Stairs

While pathways are vital for movement through gardens, lighting them to a bright level is typically not needed. Humans see vertical elements like walls, hedges, sculptures, fountains, buildings, trees, shrubs before they see horizontal surfaces including pathways and stairs. Lighting on the vertical surfaces adds to the human comfort level, especially, but not only, in spaces new to us.

Having studied Latin for multiple years, then switching to Greek with my high school classic language teacher when no more Latin courses were offered, I learned how important it is to understand when to break the rules. Much of life is learning when it is appropriate to move away from rules.

In lighting of paths, if there is a need to warn people about obstacles, such as uneven steps or guiding people through a space via a way that they may not know, then I will increase the lighting on a path to increase a sense of safety – as I did at the drop-off path at Far Niente #4 photo on page 28. This is another example of an entertainment garden in Northern California where this side path is often used by the serving staff.

I don't always light the driveway at the arrival of a business or residence. The project in PA, as seen on the next page, is an example of this. The trees in the middle and lower photos flank the driveway, and the higher light at the entry draws the guests in past those trees to reach the parking located close to the house. It makes a beautiful scene with the plant material framing that water feature and the entry door.

The close-up photos of those trees show the use of multiple uplights in front for all the trees, with downlights used to light the inside of the multiple trunked tree and gently identify the ground plane.

Design Intuition Takes Over: Honing the Art
SECTION II

Sculpting Elements – Paths, Walkways, and Stairs

Design Intuition Takes Over: Honing the Art
SECTION II
Sculpting Elements – Paths, Walkways, and Stairs

In Villanova, PA you arrive at this French chateau style home through this driveway allée. Driving through this space is ethereal, as you saw on page 33. While it seems like simply a driveway, it is such an amazing space that guests often walk the allée with the owners just for the experience. You will note there is no lighting on the driveway. When surrounded with light on your two sides, with all that light above you and with a relatively smooth surface you're walking along, no additional lighting is necessary. This idea is something we need to incorporate in more settings.

The four photos on the right page are 2006 winter, upper left; 2007 fall, upper right; 2011 spring, lower left. All three of these are old technology – halogen MR16 lamps. Then at lower right we had changed to LED in summer 2013.

At each tree we use a pair of fixtures. One aimed toward the trunk with a low wattage 36° flood and the other aimed to the center of the canopy above the road with a 25° beam. That layout did not change when we switched to LED, but the wattage did. It went down by 50% and more. Yet you can see how the color – now 3K LED – is too cold on the trunks and, while the canopy looks beautiful, the dreamy feeling has become quite crisp.

Design Intuition Takes Over: Honing the Art
SECTION II

Sculpting Elements – Paths, Walkways, and Stairs

I have wondered many times if I should have used two color temperatures, with 27°K on the trunks, and whether I should have lowere the wattage, at least on the trunks. The clients like it and they didn't want me to fuss any more, and they make the decisions. This is looking away from the house. On the next page, you'll see looking toward it.

Design Intuition Takes Over: Honing the Art
SECTION II
Sculpting Elements – Paths, Walkways, and Stairs

Looking back to the house, you see a window above the front door. That is 'his' home office window. When we initially finished the lighting in the early 2000s, I said to him 'the first time it snows, go up to your office and look at the allée.' He called me at midnight one night in awe of his allée in snow!

Upper left is fall 2011 halogen and upper right is spring 2013 3K LED. Looking this direction, the trunks look better to me and I still vacillate over which I think is better. Both have their benefits and drawbacks. And we have to move on, as LED is making old technology obsolete.

At left, this lawn beyond the cut in the hedge, (refer back to pages 53-54 for the view from inside the house), is lit with the downlight from the high trees lighting the hedge.

That lit lawn connects the back patio to the hedge. This is one of George's favorite photos of this property. He always takes many more than I ask for – always beautiful and educational to us designers.

Design Intuition Takes Over: Honing the Art
SECTION II

Sculpting Elements – Paths, Walkways, and Stairs

In Westchester County, NY, this property spreads out. Roads and walking paths move you from one activity space to another. While I still didn't light the roads, I did light features along the way to give you an idea of your progress getting to your destination or your location in the site.

As with most projects, my introduction to the site was with the client. Normally we walk, as we did that day, but it started with a drive for me to experience how people typically arrive.

There are multiple places that required identification at night – not least, the covered horse arena that the owner lets many friends and neighbors use.

What we are looking at from the car in the photo at left, is the last gate before you turn to the right to travel the newly planted allée, the final approach to the house.

On the left, through the gate, is his mom's home. There are many places to discover here.

Design Intuition Takes Over: Honing the Art
SECTION II
Sculpting Elements – Paths, Walkways, and Stairs

Just out of site in that previous daytime shot is the tree at the right, as shown in the upper photo. It is the only thing you would see as you come up the hill to the crest in that photo. I needed to identify elements like this tree that needed to become part of the lighting, as we swooped around the site.

You can see that the road curves to the left and that the gate is in front of you. The photo above is looking at the gate moving towards the house. I lit some of the big trees near the gate, but softer than that first tree and softer than the allée ahead. I also used downlight to show the stone walls, the fence, and the gate. The conifer, above, was included for visual transportation – providing visual connection along the approach.

The photo at left shows you the gate as you leave. Having traversed the property earlier with headlights on the car, the client and I agreed to not include any further lighted clues on the way out. There always becomes a limit either to scope, budget or both.

Design Intuition Takes Over: Honing the Art
SECTION II

Sculpting Elements – Paths, Walkways, and Stairs

This photo is the newly planted allée on your way to the main house. These are very different trees from the PA allée, pages 32, 76 – 78. This client saw that allée in *Forbes* magazine and wanted an allée like it.

Differences between the two projects include the fact that all the space around this allée is very private. While large, the trees were very young compared to the hundred plus year-old PA trees – the canopy had not yet knitted together over the road. These circumstances forced me to treat this allée differently, at least at the beginning.

Another difference was that there was no ground cover into which to tuck stake mount fixtures, and with a view all the way around the allée, it just made sense to use below grade fixtures.

Each tree has multiple fixtures around the outside edge of the canopy, and one near the trunk on the driveway side, to visually tie the canopy to the ground. The canopies did not yet touch side-to-side either, but they would within a few years. So fixtures for each canopy at the edge or outside the canopy would work to knit them together as the trees matured.

The middle photo is from 2016, eight years after that initial lighting installation, and you can see that the canopy has started to knit together and that the lighting does cover its entirety.

I planned that from the beginning but you will note that, unlike the PA allée, the center is not the brightest. This canopy is lit more as one overall element, leading you to the home's entry door.

Unlike the Ohio project, we didn't have to plan power distribution and load for additional fixtures and transformers. We might have to change lamping over time, but hopefully no additional fixtures will be required.

Landscape lighting doesn't end after aiming/focusing an installed plan. As plants grow their form can change; seasons show plants differently, and people seem to like to keep making changes in their gardens over time.

Design Intuition Takes Over: Honing the Art
SECTION II
Sculpting Elements – Paths, Walkways, and Stairs

George always takes amazing additional photos. This is one that shows how this allée looks like one big element and then, at the left, back down the road, you can see the tree elements that helped lead you in.

This project has a second existing allée, a side walkway between the owner's mother's house and the main house. I lit the trees slightly brighter, due to the older age of the woman who would mostly use it. There is no additional walkway lighting until the end of the allée where path lights start, as the path turns and goes to the main house front entry.

Design Intuition Takes Over: Honing the Art
SECTION II
Sculpting Elements – Structures

Often structures are the only thing lit in a scene. If any structure can hold its own, it is this carillon tower on Evening Island at the Chicago Botanic Garden (CBG). I wanted to light the planting around it providing a visual base or framework, as it would be seen by visitors from across the lake sitting on the lawn during bell concerts.

Design Intuition Takes Over: Honing the Art
SECTION II
Sculpting Elements – Structures

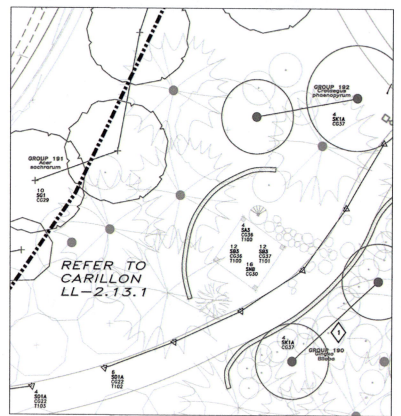

Viewed from a lawn across the lake, the carillon tower stands by itself on Evening Island. Three levels of bells can be seen as well as heard during concerts.

During conceptual design, Jan Moyer Design (JMD) presented visuals of various aspects of the complete lighting to the CBG Board. The proposal included neon strips the length of each side of the structure at the base of all four layers with bells. The idea was for guests to be able to see bell movement and the clangers producing the sounds that visitors come to hear.

Accompanying the concept drawings and proposal, JMD did mock-ups of selected elements, including the Donor Tree and the neon carillon lighting, in August, in Chicago – it was hot, humid, full of mosquitoes. See my outfit on, page 86.

Design Intuition Takes Over: Honing the Art
SECTION II
Sculpting Elements – Structures

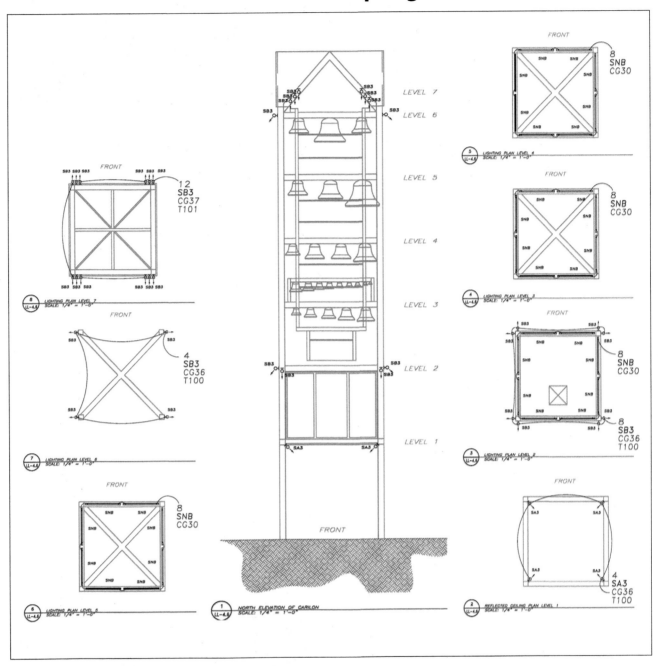

The height of the tower gave us locations to light multiple elements around the carillon scene. Starting at the level 7, at the top, groups of three low voltage adjustable fixtures were located along the angled roof line to downlight tall plantings around the tower. At levels closer to the ground, the fixtures on the outside and the inside were used to light the area immediately surrounding and under the carillon.

The best way to document this was to use an elevation plan, shown here, accompanied by a plan of each level. As you can see, on the contract and record drawings set, we referred the viewer to the details shown above for installation and maintenance.

The neon was built for me by Ben Livingston of BENEON, Austin, Texas (beneon.com). He made each piece, drove them to the Chicago site, and installed them for us. He stuck around after he completed installing the neon, because he likes to be in touch.

Design Intuition Takes Over: Honing the Art
SECTION II
Sculpting Elements – Structures

Viewers look up into the bells, so uplighting them worked great for seeing the action. Neon was chosen because it is very energy efficient and low wattage due to its high voltage – in the neighborhood of 15,000 volts. It was formed to the exact length of the tower spans, and the vibration of the bells would have minimal impact on the neon functioning.

Ben provided a housing with an asymmetrical reflector aiming the light in toward the bells. The exterior is a matte black to minimize seeing the pieces, which allowed shielding the view to the neon lamps from all perspectives.

Design Intuition Takes Over: Honing the Art
SECTION II
Sculpting Elements – Structures

No matter from where you view the tower, the contrast of value, color, and its physical height make the lit form stand out.

Focusing more closely on the action of the bells, we see that using neon as the light source, the uplighting is very even, and strong enough for the tie rods to be visible as the bells are pushed or pulled.

The tower lighting integrates that of the existing exposed bridge with the landscape lighting in between, thus completing the scene.

Design Intuition Takes Over: Honing the Art
SECTION II
Sculpting Elements – Structures

This overlook structure in Ohio is meant as a resting spot on the main house lawn. You can see to the boat house, to the main house and pool, the outdoor chapel, the birch allée gate, and, over to the distant landscapes beyond the lake.

The approach I took to this and all the exterior buildings on this property was to not actually light the building at all. Some of the buildings have decorative hanging fixtures, but, like dining chandeliers, they are more like jewelry than functional. I selected low voltage adjustable fixtures that we mounted to the structures and then lit the shoulders of the benches – to avoid light in people's eyes and to highlight the form of the furniture. We downlit plantings around the buildings and used the reflected light off the light floor paving and approaching paths to allow the buildings to glow.

Each building is similar in light level and is within the 3:1 contrast range with the brightest landscape elements so that the structures acted as beacons to help people understand where they were within the site.

Design Intuition Takes Over: Honing the Art
SECTION II
Sculpting Elements – Structures

With a large grade change from the main house lawn to the lake, stone walls with staircases supported the lake side of the overlook building. Again, the walls themselves are not lit, but using the completely shielded lights built into the walls, including the corner lights, enough light is reflected off the stone walks and stairs to softly wash the walls, which becomes a visual element completing the scene. Having that mass of lit structure helps guide people in finding their way back from remote sites. All the fixtures were made to completely hide the light source/lamp inside the housing, which has the project detail pattern etched into the copper. The multiple, 'X', pattern became a design detail used throughout the site – from the railings, to the trellis walls and light fixtures. While not all the fixtures had the pattern, the fixture shape followed the same design form.

Design Intuition Takes Over: Honing the Art
SECTION II
Sculpting Elements – Structures

At this Long Island, NY site, construction of the arrival structures, including the porte cochère and the waterfall walls with pond below, are shown under construction here. On many projects, the lighting designer needs to spend time with the team on site and at remote sites; in this case, the stone quarry. Here, so much of the structure was stone coming from one quarry and mock ups were done there on more than one occasion (see a mockup in progress and stones being cut, p.126). Understanding how all the pieces go together helps direct the lighting detailing.

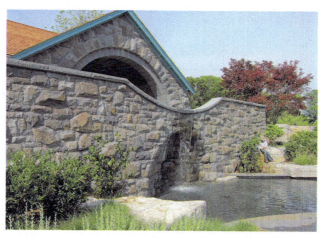

Stone is used extensively on this site. The stone masons from the New York Alcove Stone Quarry, led by Bruce O'Brien (alcovestone.com), brought tons of stone to the site and placed each stone with no mortar, using the dry stack technique. Working with landscape architect Howard Williams of Hollander Design (hollanderdesign.com), we planned lighting to show the beauty of building design, the stone and the stone work, integrated with the surrounding landscapes.

The covered entry melds into the porte cochère and that blends into the upper pool. Next, water falls over the curved edge of the wall cap into the lower pond. Each portion of these combined structures required differing lighting techniques. Some of the surrounding plants were uplit to cast shadows onto the walls flanking the lower pond, as in the upper photo on the next page. Adjustable stake mount fixtures placed at the outside edges of the lower pond are aimed to catch the waterfall and reveal the curved wall behind it at night.

The quarry stone cap, smooth on the under side but rough on the top and front, creates plenty of air bubbles in the falling water that catch light. Aiming light through the falls from the sides accentuates the water and allows the beam spread to catch that indented wall shape behind the falls.

The face of the porte cochère combines the same stone made smooth at the bottom of the curve and still rough on the face. We lit this with two stake mount adjustable fixtures aimed to the apex of the roof at a grazing location to create strong shadows balancing brightnesses throughout this mini-scene.

Design Intuition Takes Over: Honing the Art
SECTION II

Sculpting Elements – Structures

The interactive play of rough and smooth texture defined the structure's shape and aided in forming interesting lighting effects.

Originally, I had planned underwater fixtures for the fall, but, as Howard developed his ideas, he considered having plants in the lower pool. Water bodies with soil for plants presents the problem that the water will look murky when lit, so I happily switched to fixtures outside the water (my normal preference!).

Design Intuition Takes Over: Honing the Art
SECTION II
Sculpting Elements – Structures

The smooth stone lines all four opening curves at the porte cochère and I lit the stone the same way on all four outside surfaces. This reveals the curve, provides shadowing to show the stone patterning above the opening and catches the roof line, using one stake mount per curve side. The structure looks stunning after dark.

To make the scene complete and balance those strong effects on the stone, I more softly uplit the two smaller trees flanking this opening and the much larger tree on the other side, on the homes' entry side. Then, I grazed the evergreens through the porte cochère as a view that is at the brightness level of the structure.

Design Intuition Takes Over: Honing the Art
SECTION II
Sculpting Elements – Structures

Within the curves are still rough but softened stone. Each of the four corners is lit with pairs of stake mount uplights set at a 10–20° aiming angle to graze the stone and follow the curve. Each of the individual elements add up to make the overall scene.

Design Intuition Takes Over: Honing the Art
SECTION II
Sculpting Elements – Structures

With openings on four sides, I had to provide a strong view through them all. The view beyond the upper pond as guests leave the front door at night, and the forest, enhanced with new trees, is right along the road. Uplighting the new trees casts softer light onto the existing mature trees and provides a visual destination to complete the scene, while hiding the road.

Design Intuition Takes Over: Honing the Art
SECTION II
Sculpting Elements – Structures

Little details throughout the site hold the individual scenes together. At the edge of the front forest, (lower left, previous page), you get a close-up of that view through the porte cochère.

Above is a secret passage from the front garden to the parking area. I lit the stone around the opening similarly, but a little softer than the porte cochère, as you can sometimes see them at the same time.

At left, you can see custom outdoor floor lamps that coordinate with the sconces on the house, but with much better shielding of the light source. These are used on the back patio that is large and has no way to easily light it. This kind of decorative fixture has usage in many garden patios. It requires strength and heavy weight to avoid tipping over. Note in the daytime photo that we put a copper mesh over the diffuse glass to soften the glass effect. The decision to have a lit glass instead of keeping it completely shielded had to do with providing good horizontal/general light across the patio showing peoples bodies and faces.

Design Intuition Takes Over: Honing the Art
SECTION II
Sculpting Elements – Structures

Design Intuition Takes Over: Honing the Art
SECTION II
Sculpting Elements – Structures

This last structure in this section is a special and emotional one. This barn belongs to a friend of my cousin's ex-husband, Doug. He served our country and felt strongly about our lost soldiers and the MIA (missing in action). He asked his friend if he could make a homage to them on her barn. All the parts, the eagle weather vane, the signs, the lighting equipment, all the installation, and, my design, were all donated to Doug. He was getting a donated kidney from my cousin in an attempt to keep him alive.

I asked HK Lighting for 20-watt stake mount floods and tested them on the back of George's NY studio – about the same size as the barn, (photo lower left). Knowing that two fixtures would do it, we jumped on a plane and got the barn lit just before Doug's surgery. Within minutes, passing cars starting tooting their horns, exactly what Doug wanted. We got a photo to him before his surgery and for the few years he survived afterwards, he got to enjoy this tribute.

Mock ups are critical to making sure lighting works. Sometimes, moving a fixture a couple of inches creates an amazing effect, which you wouldn't *have* otherwise. Sometimes moving a fixture three feet doesn't matter at all. Lighting is complicated. Even after 45 years of practice, I learn so much every time I take the time to play with a new fixture, a new light source, or a new situation. Do we get paid for this effort? Sometimes yes, sometimes no, and, in my opinion, that doesn't matter. We are never done learning, and, I know everyone has really busy lives, but, knowing what to do and how to do it best is part of our responsibility in our business.

Plus, it's fun! I know we have to spend a lot of time in the dark, at night, but if we don't, we'll miss some incredible opportunity to create something amazing, and that can help someone – isn't that why we do thi?

Design Intuition Takes Over: Honing the Art
SECTION II
Sculpting Elements – Art

From the beginning I have loved lighting sculptures – even ones I don't like (There have been many). But always, light makes them different from their daytime appearance, and often better.

This multi-piece sculpture was made by my dear friend, Ben Livingston. Neither of us can remember if I asked him to make the three metal sculptures of, "me", and the two Salukis, plus the incredible neon bone that I did ask Ben to make. It lived in our NY forest for many years. We had to have Ben remake the neon bone a couple times when branches fell on it.

The Salukis show better in the winter snows and the bone melts its own snow cave. It doesn't take much heat, and neon doesn't produce much, so the melted snow around the bone was a much appreciated happenstance that taught me to turn on your landscape lighting when a big snowstorm starts. Light can only get through a couple feet of snow pack that stays on the ground, but given time it can melt, even LED can melt – a lot of snow.

Design Intuition Takes Over: Honing the Art
SECTION II
Sculpting Elements – Art

Tony Lato installed this Connecticut project and took these photos of this small part of the property. When you first look at that massive tree, upper left, you have to look closely at the left side to see the full size sculpture.

I lit the sculpture using one downlight mounted in the tree. The fixture is about 20'/6 meters above the ground on the left trunk. I believe sculptures tell you how to light them. With the torso bending back to the tree and the left leg extended, lighting this sculpture from above and from the right allows the light to accentuate all the body features. It also creates that fabulous shadow in the snow.

The lamp was probably a very narrow spot, using Halogen MR16s back then, in the early 2000s, it was probably an OSI (Osram Sylvania) 37 watt, 10° lamp. In landscape lighting, over the years, I found very few times to use 'tight spot' lamps in Halogen MR16, 10° was about as tight as they every got. Very long throws are when we might use spots in landscape lighting. It is rare to need one.

Also in Connecticut, Tony helped with the aiming of this project. Your are met coming down a very long, remote driveway by this Rodan boar sculpture. In the left photo you see a tree lit way in the distance, at the end of the right side of the drive, to avoid a dark hole in your view. Then you see bright light at the left – the visual cue to go in that direction to arrive at the home's entry.

The boar is lit with two ring mount downlights. One over his head is the brightest of the three elements. The second downlight over his back end assures that all the anatomy the artist thought important is clearly visible. The third, and perhaps most important light, is a ground recessed uplight to show you his snout. Without that uplight the front of his nose would be in shadow.

Design Intuition Takes Over: Honing the Art
SECTION II
Sculpting Elements – Art

Animal sculptures are in many gardens. These three are downlit and you can see how good that makes them look, even when not all of the sculpture has light. The rabbit has one fixture over her cotton tail and one doing from her ears to her front toes. The bird is lit with one fixture mounted in the palm that also covers the trunk and that amazing wall detail, as well as making the bird stand out. The dog, above top, is lit from a branch above/behind him.

Design Intuition Takes Over: Honing the Art
SECTION II
Sculpting Elements – Art

This man sculpture has a bird landing on his hand for a drink of water. His outstretched hand helps people navigate this garden, and serves as the focal point from the outdoor dining table. The planting around him changed over the years, as did the light source from Halogen to LED.

On the first page In section three, page 189, we'll see how this all changed in the mid 2010's when the property owners bought back a parcel previous owners had sold off, probably mid last century, and the entire back landscape changed.

Design Intuition Takes Over: Honing the Art
SECTION II
New Water Technique – Shore Scraping

As the years passed, I learned more about creating a stable composition through balancing brightnesses across a scene for all reasons, as well as how to best light multiple kinds of elements I had been lighting all along. Then came the field of grass on Evening Island. The upper left photo shows part of the original mock-up for the CBG board to approve the conceptual design and for us to move on directly to contract documents... But, you notice that the entire front of the island to the left of the carillon is dark except for the very back of the island.

The upper right and lower left photos show the extent of the grass fields. To create a cohesive view from across the lake, I had to figure out how to light the width of the grass along the expanse of the island to connect the left, right, and back parts of the view or scene.

I created a new lighting technique that I call, shore-scraping, It consists of fixtures in a body of water, with the fixture head above the water, requiring the fixture to have a new (at that time) rating called wet-dry. This essentially is a submersible fixture in construction, but one that does not rely on the water to cool the fixture/lamp and can be completely submersed for some time, ie., in a flood, but not permanently submersed in a water feature. In the lower right photo you see the pair on 'this' side of the shore and there is a corresponding pair on the other side.

At this project, the fixture pairs cross aim the island, using the expansive distance to create the appearance I needed. Top photo, next page shows the daytime island; then the lighting without the shore-scraping and the lower photo shows the complete lighting. You can clearly see how important that fill light layer is in the cohesion of this view.

Tom Williams, of the eight-member aiming team, agreed to go into the lake and set those fixtures for me.

Design Intuition Takes Over: Honing the Art
SECTION II
New Water Technique – Shore Scraping

I had confirmed a lake level cut-off system with CBG that turned off all fixtures that would be swamped in a big flood event. The most important detail of this system was the control scene in the event that people would be on the island; there are four control buttons, and, this one turned off the shore scraping. There is no way to shield shore scraping from a path on the island.

Design Intuition Takes Over: Honing the Art
SECTION II

New Water Technique – Shore Scraping

In Ohio, the lake you see in the upper photo is a man-made lake. The husband, working with the landscape architect, originally had requested two lakes, and, was allowed one in the end. From the lower photo, you, can see that landscape designer Martin Koepke (513-561-7379), brought in big boulders and rocks and created a bank from the normal lake level up to the pathway level. Again, we had a water-level controls system in place. Because of the bank at the far end of the lake from the boat house, implementing shore-scraping connected the landscape at the bank-top to the water level.

Martin planned multiple combinations of rocks/water plantings along the shoreline, creating a beautiful lake edge. This was just planted... imagine after the plants grow up. Lighting designers have to imagine and plan for this.

Design Intuition Takes Over: Honing the Art
SECTION II

New Water Technique – Shore Scraping

In the upper photo you can see that the level change is several foot/1m+ from water to path level. Without lighting on the bank, it would visually disconnect the overall lighting effect, as you will see on the next page. This system had about eight wet-dry fixtures sprinkled along the line of that end of the lake. Again, Tom Williams was one of the people in the lake placing the fixtures. We tried to keep them amongst the rocks and plantings. From a distance, they are not easily seen. Like the initial CBG installation, the fixtures need to be aimed at 90° off zenith (straight up) to produce the lighting effect needed.

This Ohio site has wildlife, including this goose who approved our fixture locations. A two-page comparison, next page, includes a daytime photo, one without shore-scraping, and finally, the lighting with shore-scraping. It not only connects the lake level, but fills in some depth at path level, and must be turned off when walking the shoreline.

Design Intuition Takes Over: Honing the Art
SECTION II
New Water Technique – Shore Scraping

Design Intuition Takes Over: Honing the Art
SECTION II
New Water Technique – Shore Scraping

Design Intuition Takes Over: Honing the Art
SECTION II
Project Challenges – Rooftops – City HOA and Power Distribution

Over time we all see interesting issues. In Manhattan, I was retained to light a rooftop garden in a building run by the Homeowners Association, as many are in NYC.

The apartment was about 500 square feet and the gardens about four times that size. The owner, Enid, was very interested in gardening and wanted to feel like she was continually in her garden space.

These three photos are from the kitchen, her office table (next to her bed), and from the main room. No matter where she is, she has a connection to her garden.

Doing the downlighting for her space was easy, after getting approval from the HOA. We ran power along the roof line and had fixtures attached to the building as needed.

The uplighting would continually change as Enid developed the garden and made new decisions about what worked in the unusual location for plants, all in pots. We needed a system that could easily adapt and be changed as the garden evolved.

Design Intuition Takes Over: Honing the Art
SECTION II

Project Challenges – Rooftops – City HOA and Power Distribution

Here is Don Bradley, on Enid's roof lamping a fixture during the aiming session. Of course, the second light that you see is his headlamp.

Once a fixture is aimed producing the desired effect, the fixture is tightened to hold the aim, then the glare shield is set and locked to block direct view of the lamp.

While we needed the views from indoor to outdoor to work for Enid, we also needed the outdoor space to work. She would spend time on that patio even in the dead of winter. The downlighting is all aimed at plants, furniture settings, and other interesting aspects that also change.

All directions lead to views overlooking the Manhattan cityscape, (right, page 108). A wonderful daily experience to have and one that needed to be incorporated into the lighting of this personal landscape. Once again, in my work there is no path lighting and, yet you can see your way around the space easily and comfortably.

Shadows through plants from the downlighting helps break up the space, making the long narrow spaces feel more comfortable as you look across or walk through them. Don and I loved our time up on the roof with her!

Design Intuition Takes Over: Honing the Art
SECTION II

Project Challenges – Rooftops – City HOA and Power Distribution

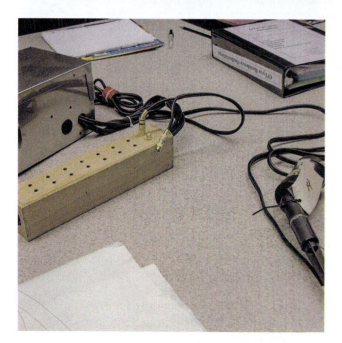

No downlighting was specifically aimed onto the dining table, that would be augmented with real or LED candles. When starting on this, we considered using quick disconnects throughout (lower left). But, Enid came up with this raised floor decking (lower right) that allowed us to easily reconfigure the power distribution as it was needed.

Design Intuition Takes Over: Honing the Art
SECTION II

Project Challenges – Lighting Long Distances

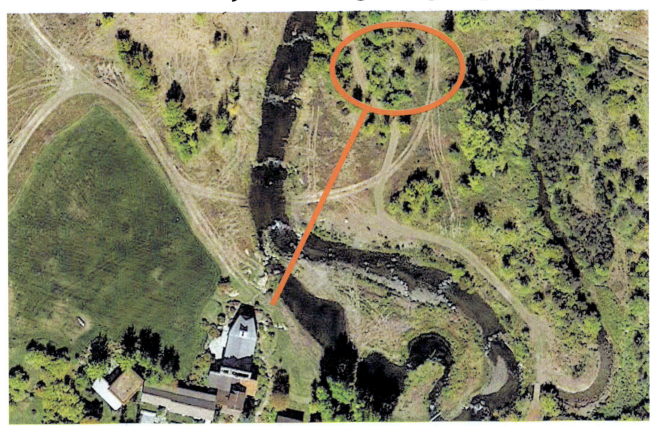

Located in Gunnison, CO, this 15,000 acre/6000+ hectare property has a smoking porch at one end of the main house, (pages 114-115). The owner wanted a view for when he and his friends relaxed and told stories of the day. Flanking the river are some willow shrubs and across the river, quite a ways off, is this copse of Populus deltoides/Cottonwood trees.

Design Intuition Takes Over: Honing the Art
SECTION II

Project Challenges – Lighting Long Distances

The drawing on the nextpage shows that we lit the copse of trees only from the front. Around 200'/61m away, it only took between 20–35 watt halogen lamps. The beam spreads were predominantly 60° with a few at 36°. It doesn't take much light, and reflector halogen lamps could easily reach to the top of tall trees, shown here. The same is true with the LED replacement (sometimes called, 'drop-in'), lamps or integral modules.

Walking the distance, George captured this reflection in the still water in front of the trees. That kind of reflection isn't seen from the porch because of the action of the river.

Design Intuition Takes Over: Honing the Art
SECTION II

Project Challenges – Lighting Long Distances

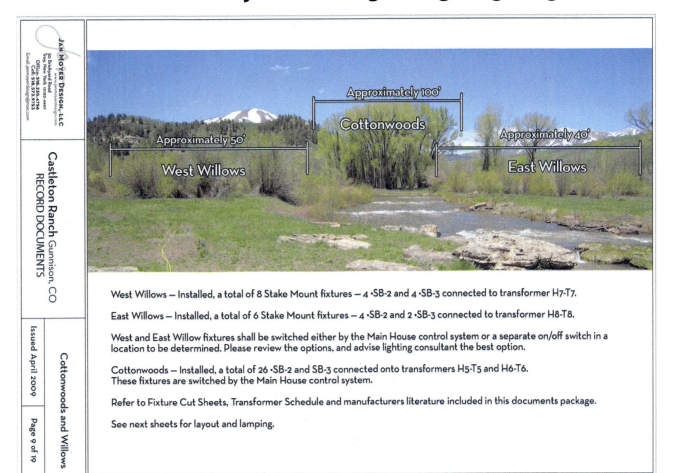

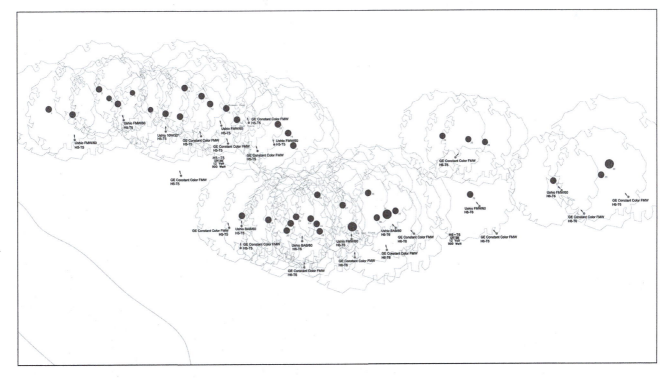

Design Intuition Takes Over: Honing the Art
SECTION II

Project Challenges – Lighting Long Distances

This gives you a view of the porch under construction and then a completed view of the lighting, at right. You also see all our extension cords for the conceptual design mockup we did for the owners. Below, you see the lighting plan we installed at the eaves of the porch. The plan on the next page shows the lighting planned for the rocks and the grasses that would get planted.

An interesting detail of this is that those 20-watt halogen lamps we used for the nearby rocks are some of the same lamps we used on the Cottonwood trees.

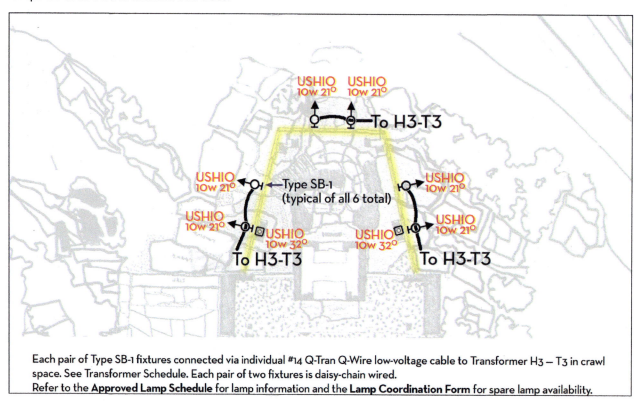

Each pair of Type SB-1 fixtures connected via individual #14 Q-Tran Q-Wire low-voltage cable to Transformer H3 – T3 in crawl space. See Transformer Schedule. Each pair of two fixtures is daisy-chain wired.
Refer to the **Approved Lamp Schedule** for lamp information and the **Lamp Coordination Form** for spare lamp availability.

Design Intuition Takes Over: Honing the Art
SECTION II
Project Challenges – Lighting Long Distances

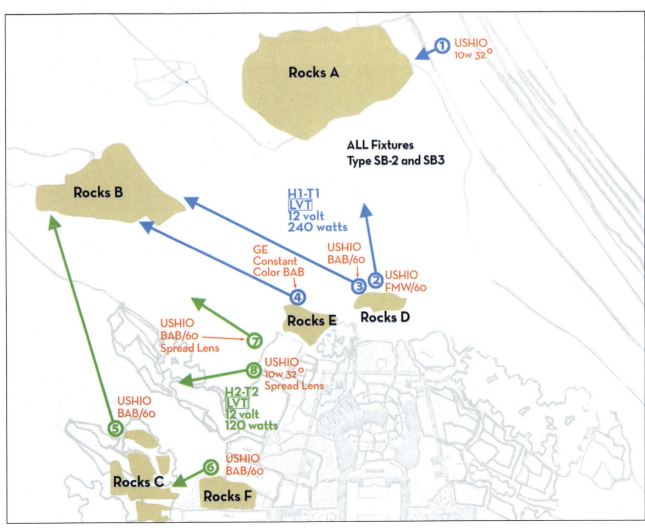

Design Intuition Takes Over: Honing the Art
SECTION II

Project Challenges – Lighting Long Distances

Photography can't show the sense of the actual distance. About a football field separates the lighting on the rocks at the porch from the Cottonwoods. You would guess that it would take a lot of light to, 'show', the Cottonwoods and the Willows, but it just doesn't.

Design Intuition Takes Over: Honing the Art
SECTION II

Project Challenges – Lighting Long Distances

My first view of this large South Carolina property was just after the Christmas holidays. The owner is removing the red bows from the brick columns that introduce the road into this property.

At that entry, he wanted us to announce the entrance. We had to be very careful; a neighbor drove by while we were aiming the lights and warned us that the lighting better not be too bright.

We mounted two fixtures in the right tree with one lighting the left column and planting surrounding it, and the second lighting the right column and it's plantings. I love the lit Tillandsia usneoides/Spanish Moss hanging from the branches, completing the entry view. Then a few trees in we had two more fixtures. Without any more lighting, you would think that arriving guests would have to rely on their car headlights.

Actually, we introduced enough mini-scenes along the way that the lighting directs you in and, like signage, advises you of decisions you might need to make along the way.

The husband wanted this lighting – the wife wasn't on board initially. By the end, she was planning walking cocktail parties.

Design Intuition Takes Over: Honing the Art
SECTION II
Project Challenges – Lighting Long Distances

In the upper photo you can see a turnoff toward the caretaker's cottage, and, in the distance, another visual scene. At each turning option, I used downlight to get attention.

At the locations we decided to provide lighting, there would be a decision to make about direction to continue, or creating a mini-scene to help guide you along the way.

At each scene, we used the quantity of fixtures needed to show the trees, form, including the branching structure and the canopy. In the left photo you see the shadow of a tree we chose not to light at this location.

I wanted people to see the nature of these Southern Oaks with their hanging moss and their expansive reaching form. The day and night photos of, 'Tree 35', shows that we didn't light them evenly, yet we showed their massive nature. One low branch extends into the pond behind it. One afternoon, as we were preparing the lighting for aiming that night, we were joined by an alligator making sure we did things correctly.

I am always amazed that we lit 'Tree 35', with only 12 fixtures.

Design Intuition Takes Over: Honing the Art
SECTION II
Project Challenges – Lighting Long Distances

Tree 35

Design Intuition Takes Over: Honing the Art
SECTION II

Project Challenges – Lighting Long Distances

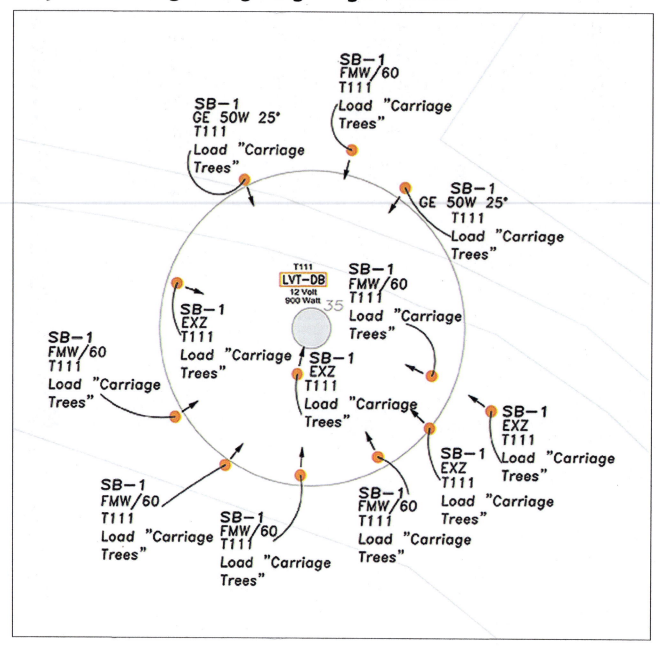

Located at that turn-off point to the caretakers, Tree 35 served as a guidepost the owner could mention to arriving guests, along with other visual cues that they would see on their way to arrive at the main house. The road runs straight toward the main house to the point you see in the upper right photo, then it makes a circle to drop guests, go to the parking area off to the right, and return back to the distant road.

I used the trees in front of the house to hold fixtures creating that soft swath of light on the ground plane in front of the house. Then I uplit trees both left and right to frame the view.

A view to the left of the house, that you would see from the screened porch (left side of the house), is shown in the lower left photo, next page. Look carefully, and you'll see the arborist moving the lift truck into position. In the right photo you can see the four fixtures he is about to install in that tree to create a distant view from the screened porch. The fixtures are prewired and he has the tools to attach the fixtures, pre-aim and set the glare shields, in preparation for our night adjustments, along with the screws and cable ties for the wires coming down the tree.

Design Intuition Takes Over: Honing the Art
SECTION II

Project Challenges – Lighting Long Distances

Design Intuition Takes Over: Honing the Art
SECTION II

Project Challenges – Lighting Long Distances

The upper photo shows how I sculpted the shore line with those four fixtures put into that one tree: two aimed along the left and back shore line, and two onto the palm and right shoreline to create the scene.
The lower photo is the view from the porch, and you can even see reflections in the water. The idea was to express the expanse of this property, even as it is located not very far from town.

Design Intuition Takes Over: Honing the Art
SECTION II

Project Challenges – Issues When Lighting a Tight Space

Landscape Architect, Howard Williams of Edmund D. Hollander Landscape Architect Design (hollanderdesign.com), imagined the rain wall with a simple drip. Located one level below the north end of the pool patio and just outside the exercise room, all fixtures had to be hidden to avoid glare. The rain wall sits merely 6" in front of the back wall – it is a very tight space. The project started in 2009 – a time when LED technology in architectural lighting products was still evolving rapidly, but had not advanced to meet this challenge with certainty. Yet there really was no other way to go.

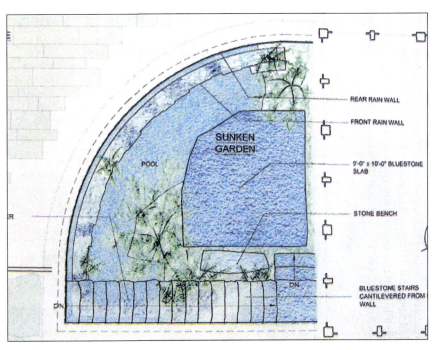

Howard imagined this as a contemplation space. To create that sense took careful planning. The plan, above right, shows a set of stairs providing entry from the pool deck level. A large blue stone slab serves as the 'patio' surrounded by a shallow pool. Glass windows and doors, the width of the patio, provide an amazing view during exercise.

The rain wall has planters and water pockets sculpted out of stones taken from the quarry, (alcovestone.com), in Upstate New York, for this and the entire site. Surrounding the patio slab, several pockets have additional planting. Mounted under that Blue stone slab patio are several sets of the fixtures shown above left. The fixture pair sit just above the water line and had to be able to aim as needed under the stone. Three sets of these are used for grazing the face of the entire rain wall. The upper fixture lights further up and the lower lights the base of the rain wall.

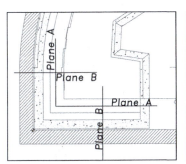
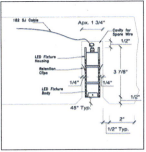

A series of drawings, prepared as part of the contract documents, shows how every fixture recesses into specific stones, where and how each fixture fits into each stone, and how each fixture tilts for aiming. Individual stones were core drilled at the quarry. Individual cables, labeled at each end and fitted with gold quick disconnect fittings, allowed fixtures to recess in the stone a half inch with the surrounding stone chamfered at 45° for shielding and light distribution.

Design Intuition Takes Over: Honing the Art
SECTION II

Project Challenges – Issues When Lighting a Tight Space

This elevation had to provide enough information for the stone masons to understand fixture locations, and for the electrical contractor to install the fixtures with proper connections allowing removal for maintenance. A plan could not show this needed information. Two transformer locations called Power Supply A and B, at opposite ends of the splayed wall, originate power distribution throughout the wall. Individual cables had to feed down to the base of the wall, travel horizontally to enter a stone drilled exactly to create a pathway to each fixture, and then travel up to each fixture location. The red lines indicate cable paths starting from the Power Supplies.

Design Intuition Takes Over: Honing the Art
SECTION II

Project Challenges – Issues When Lighting a Tight Space

The owners had requested a rain wall and, having never previously had one, insisted that it be mocked up to see the wall and ensure that the rain wall made them fall in love with it. During the testing landscape architect Howard Williams adjusted the flow of water to get the drip he had experienced on a hike in Upstate New York. The lighting recessed into stones of the front wall provides lighting to the back wall to help open that space between walls. To graze the front of the wall, additional lights were located under the stone patio slab in the surrounding pool. Unlike the original mock-up at the quarry, we decided to limit the grazing to the lower level of the wall for two reasons. First, to not detract from the lighting of the water basins, falling water, plants, and back wall. Second, we didn't want any glare visible to people at the main pool deck level looking over the railing into the rain wall area.

After some of the stones had been removed from the quarry, a section of the wall was set up inside one of the quarry buildings. Howard is reviewing the wall with the owners and then the building lights were turned off. The proposed lighting of the back wall, planting pockets, and the wall face were shown for approval. With client approval, work could continue. One owner turned to his wife and whispered, 'This is Art'.

Design Intuition Takes Over: Honing the Art
SECTION II

Project Challenges – Issues When Lighting a Tight Space

Each required stone had to be extracted from the quarry and cut to the appropriate size, then labeled to ensure proper eventual placement in the wall. This process continued over many months. Once all the stones had been prepared, a full-scale mock up was to be made, still at the quarry. This would show what the wall would actually look like to the owners and to the entire design team. Stones coming out of the quarry didn't necessarily match the landscape architect's specifications, so as the wall came together, the stone masons kept the lighting needs detailed on the issued drawings in mind.

As the wall rose off the ground, the masons determined that some fixture locations required slight adjustments in order to achieve our lighting goals. Of the dozens of fixtures, only two required moving, according to the masons. Here we are discussing fixtures that required movement. The stone mason points out an original fixture location from the plans, and I am pointing at his suggested relocation, taking into account the aiming, the path light needed to travel, and its destination. Each location that would not work would affect the success of the overall lighting composition for the wall. Each location was critical and *only* the documents allowed the mason to ensure that outcome.

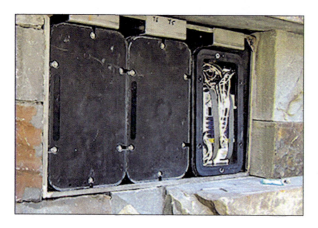

All the power originated from transformers recessed in waterproof compartments inside the wall with removable matching stone face plates. Each transformer was installed with a tiltable plate for access to the back of its wiring vault for any maintenance required in the future.

Design Intuition Takes Over: Honing the Art
SECTION II

Project Challenges – Issues When Lighting a Tight Space

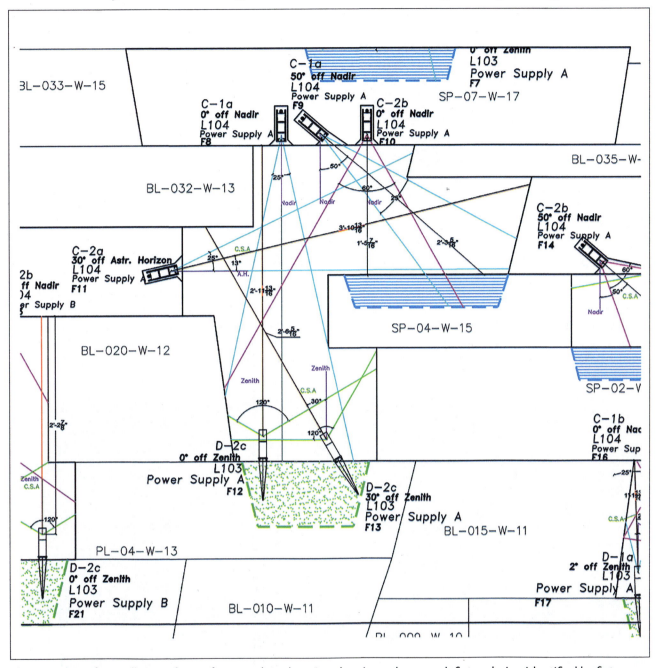

This snapshot of a small area of one of many other elevation drawings, shows each fixture being identified by fixture type, its aiming off either zenith, nadir, or astronomic horizon (either to the left or right, depending on degree number), control load number, transformer location, and a fixture number. In addition, using colored lines we showed the area that the specified beam spread, as indicated, would cover. Then, inside each beam spread, we indicated the main candlepower throw, including the throw length, which allowed us to calculate the brightness at each location. This drawing shows that, in this case, the uplights have a different control load number from the downlights. This allowed setting the dimming to achieve the brightness balance we imagined.

While this data was prepared for lighting purposes, it was this information that informed the masons as to the success of our original locations. Without this information provided to them, and their careful attention to it, the lighting may not have been so successful. This was a herculean effort in my office, and we can only applaud the masons for their efforts to pay attention, to understand our goals, and to help us achieve them in this challenging construction effort.

Design Intuition Takes Over: Honing the Art
SECTION II
Project Challenges – Issues When Lighting a Tight Space

In the above construction photo, you can see the spillways at the very top of the wall and both a water basin stone and a planter stone.

Just above the stairs, notice the stones cut with holes to hold the stair light fixture, page 70. Many of the stair stones hold fixtures for downlighting. At this point the electrical cables have been installed and are rolled up waiting for the fixtures to arrive for installation.

Construction of the rain wall has started, above. The roll of cable is waiting for stones to be lowered into the space and will be fed up through each layer as the wall progresses up to the pool patio level.

Viewing the rain wall had to work from the pool patio level as you descended the stairs into the space, as well as from the training room within the home. Lighting set into the stones aims toward the back wall showing the separation of the walls. Downlighting from fixtures set into the stones lights the water, the patio stone, the water basins, and the planters, both in the wall and in the surrounding area. Howard wanted a contemplation space for the owners, and they got it.

Design Intuition Takes Over: Honing the Art
SECTION II

Radical Landscape Change – Severe Planting Changes

Typically we plan for normal changes of growth at the beginning of a project. Over the course of my career, and thankfully after decades of work, so I could respond, I was presented several times with what I now call "radical" landscape change. The series of photos above is an example of one that I found in December 2005 during a normal site visit for the project.

After seeing the large tree plantings in December 2004, I returned in August 2005 to flag fixtures, once the shrubs and other plantings, except ground cover, had been at least placed. After flagging, I am standing among the new trees of the middle photo reviewing it to make sure it's all ok.

Then, when I returned in December 2005, the lower photo shows a drastically different planting condition. What a shock. Luckily, the site is large enough that all the trees and shrubs removed, got placed elsewhere on the property. You can imagine trying to rethink this scene.

As you can see in that lowest photo, all the flags are gone, and fixtures have been installed. On large projects, sometimes it's hard for clients to wrap their head around their landscape until they actually see it… and changes follow.

At this portion of this project, we were able to still use the fixtures and moved them to a different location as the project developed. It was such a big undertaking that we ordered fixtures in batches as the project progressed.

Design Intuition Takes Over: Honing the Art
SECTION II
Radical Landscape Change – Severe Planting Changes

This is a side walkway out the back of several guest buildings to the beach in the Bahamas. We uplit the palms and used the reflected light for the pathway. On one of many trips, we had been installing and aiming for about four days/nights. With only one more night, we kept working on getting this portion of the site plan installed and aimed, and then we get a call about a big change that needed to be dealt with that day.

Design Intuition Takes Over: Honing the Art
SECTION II

Radical Landscape Change – Severe Planting Changes

Here is a construction view from the beach looking back the opposite way along that beach path.

At the beach, you see trunks of two palms that were planted as per the original planting plan. Notice that we have transformers being prepared for the lighting.

The LA got a call from the owner to install more palms as a visual barrier – today. The next door property was sold and construction was starting.

Because the project was in the Bahamas and electrical equipment was not locally available, we were careful to have equipment on site.

Design Intuition Takes Over: Honing the Art
SECTION II

Radical Landscape Change – Severe Planting Changes

Multiple additional palm trees were brought in at the last minute and we flagged lights to accommodate the additional trees. Having fixtures, transformers, lamps, and all kinds of electrical supplies on site, we were able to respond to the emergency additions. The contractors unpackaged, prepped, and installed all the equipment.

The entire team worked to get everything we needed assembled and we marked up the changes on the lighting plans. Don Bradley made sure that we always had all kinds of electrical supplies and never got caught short, so we were always able to respond remotely, just as we did on projects where supplies were more available, ie., the rain wall. We needed a storage and workspace to be able to organize and retrieve all the various parts and pieces during construction. We worked with the owner's representative to make sure there would be storage space after construction ended, due to the difficulty of getting equipment at this location and the owner's need for things to be perfect at all times.

Design Intuition Takes Over: Honing the Art
SECTION II

Radical Landscape Change – Severe Planting Changes

The aiming was completed that night, the fifth night of a week of work on site – we were tired and thought we had the project under control. This kind of surprise puts a kink in plans, of course. Having documentation current, along with supplies available, makes responding possible, but then puts the plan slightly off course.

Since we were leaving Paradise Island the next morning, we had to make sure that we had everything organized on site before we left. We needed to know how this had impacted our planned work, and how we would adjust our plans to stay on course for completion.

This affected our inventory for the rest of the project, so, we had to make sure we resolved whatever additional supplies were now needed and get them on site before we returned.

Since there was a line of palms already, the addition of more didn't upset the overall composition, whew!

Design Intuition Takes Over: Honing the Art
SECTION II

Radical Landscape Change – Severe Site Changes

Arriving at this site in Bermuda, the first thing the LA and owner showed me was the model, upper left. It would become a planting wall with a grotto and a slide through the wall that opens into the pool. Along with those, the LA carefully planned the planting pockets, the stairways, the hot tub, and of course, the plants themselves. Somewhere along the process, he wasn't involved. The end result was that the wall had very little resemblance to the original plans. And, as usual, no one kept the lighting designer up to date on changes.

Design Intuition Takes Over: Honing the Art
SECTION II

Radical Landscape Change – Severe Site Changes

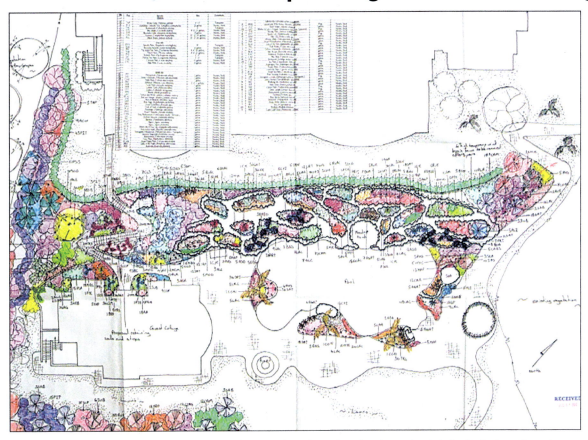

Every plant is show on the walls planting plan and listed on the planting schedule included on that plan.

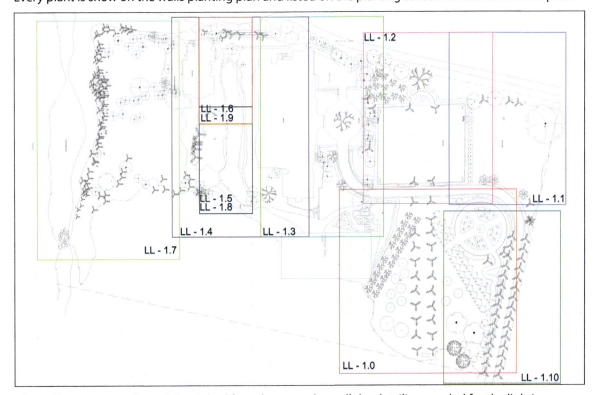

The wall was so complicated that it had four sheets to show all the detailing needed for the lighting.

Design Intuition Takes Over: Honing the Art
SECTION II

Radical Landscape Change – Severe Site Changes

Building the wall included power and water distribution lines, structural framing, and then covering the mesh with material that would withstand the hurricanes that hit the island every year.

Without the LA involved any longer, as required changes occurred no documentation was made by anyone. I got a call from the electrician saying he was trying to follow my drawings to install the transformers, but really needed my help, and could I come to Bermuda for a site visit?

Design Intuition Takes Over: Honing the Art
SECTION II

Radical Landscape Change – Severe Site Changes

This shows the just-completed wall structure. Planting had been done around the wall but there was nothing in the planting pockets as yet. The layout of the wall had changed so now our work had to change to allow completion.

My team and I started reviewing the plans with the actual site layout. There were no relationships between the two. We tried marking up our drawings to show the planting pockets as they were constructed. Jessica stood in each one with a number so that I could try and reconcile this with our drawings. As you can see, we needed the owner to consult with us at some point, as we had given up. We essentially had to start over.

This project is the one that taught me to wait to do complete documents until after we had been able to flag fixture locations. Essentially so much change happens on projects that it makes more sense to flag fixture locations and document those decisions in the field – and only then purchase equipment, so we have the right quantity and type of fixtures.

I learned to not put fixtures on contract documents. Instead, I list an estimated number of each type to be connected to a specific transformer and control load, so the project budget can be established and contractors can bid the project. Then we wait for planting of trees.

137

Design Intuition Takes Over: Honing the Art
SECTION II
Radical Landscape Change – Severe Site Changes

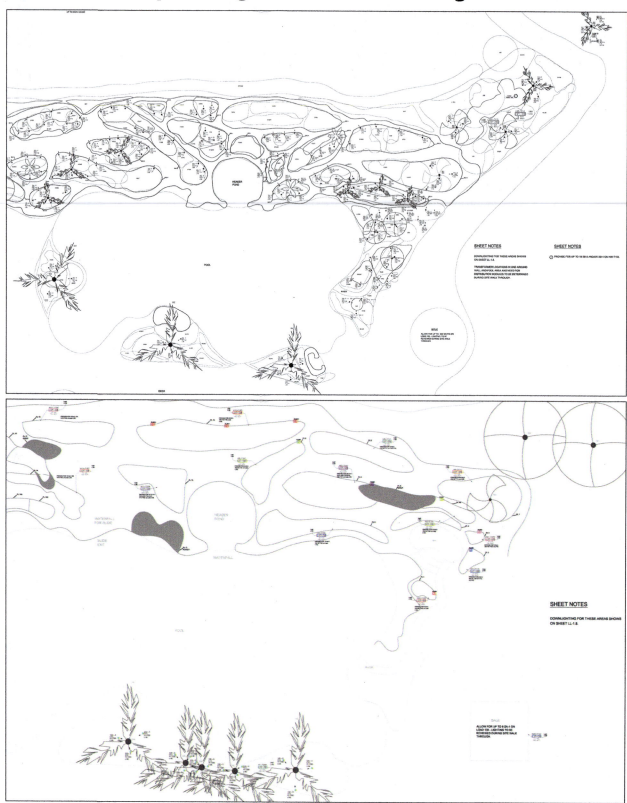

The upper drawing, from the original contract document set, shows fixture locations. After that site visit, looking at the modifications, the new drawing shows only transformer locations and distribution junction boxes. The planting plan no longer applies due to such large changes, which explains why we can only estimate fixture quantities now.

Design Intuition Takes Over: Honing the Art
SECTION II

Radical Landscape Change – Severe Site Changes

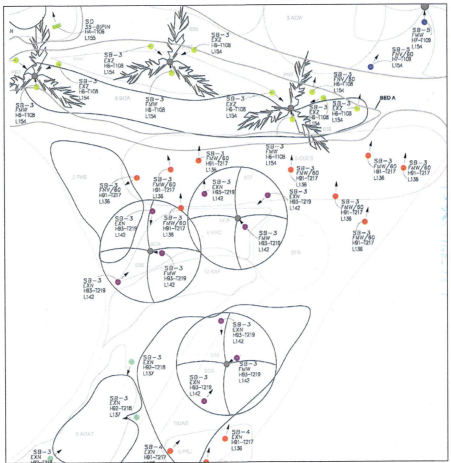

This close up shows that not only did we remove fixtures from the drawing, but had to adapt to planting pockets' changes and the relocation of the hot tub as well. It was an entirely new situation.

On the new layout we assigned new planter ID numbers, transformer and junction box locations, and the number of fixtures connected to the correct transformer and control load.

Planning this way from the beginning saves a lot of time, effort, and money.

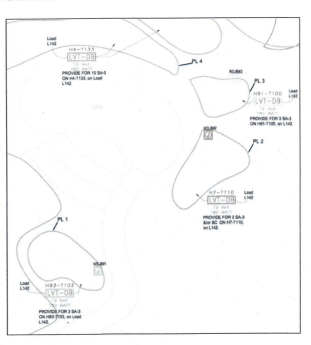

Design Intuition Takes Over: Honing the Art
SECTION II

Radical Landscape Change – Severe Site Changes

Ten years earlier at this Lafayette, CA project, two Acer palmatum/Japanese Maples flank stairs, and two Lagerstroemia indica/Crape Myrtle trees sit at the top of the hill.

Ten years later, only the second Crape Myrtle remains and the stairs have been moved. This tree, which had been only a part of the scene originally, has now become a focal point.

This was one of many changes that I observed when the owner invited me to come see the garden. He had retired and really loved his gardens, so he decided to make some changes. I asked him for a little time to simply take them in.

At the other end of the back yard, from the photos to the left, was a big Quercus agrifolia/California Live Oak that had been the focal point forever. Now it was just one of many elements in this new space with a new arbor and gate, a boccie ball court and a new guest house.

So much had changed that I had to essentially rethink the design from scratch. Then I had to assess if we had enough power distribution and start planning the new night vision of the gardens. I had to re-allocate fixtures and think about what additional fixtures were needed for all the changes.

On the next pages, you'll see the extensive changes in between the two ends of this space and all the new Japanese Maples that were planted, along with new walls and a new dry stream bed.

Design Intuition Takes Over: Honing the Art
SECTION II

Radical Landscape Change – Severe Site Changes

On page 7 you saw the original lighting of this Oak. Now, as you see, it is simply one of the elements in this much more developed space. Even though it was a big tree ten years earlier, it had grown substantially. We added lighting to it and to many other elements, including new plants, the trellis, gate, and the boccie ball court. Not small additions.

Design Intuition Takes Over: Honing the Art
SECTION II

Radical Landscape Change – Severe Site Changes

The hillside in between always had the conifers at the back and these three Prunus (species)/Cherry trees in ground cover.

With no other large plants or trees surrounding them, the Cherry trees were easily visible throughout the year, so the downlighting *needs* to be softened.

With the new walls, multiple Acer palmatum/Japanese Maples, the stream, and other plantings added, the scene had changed dramatically. The Cherries were no longer the stars of the hillside – rather they show predominantly during the day in the early spring while they are in bloom and while the Maples haven't either bloomed or pushed their new leaves. A few weeks on, next page upper photo, as the Maples start to show life, they now blend in with all the planting. Once they leaf out, along with the green-leafed Maples, the red-leafed Maples, and the stream, they are just part of the scene. This series of garden additions changed the personality of the garden. I learned we need to be prepared for all kinds of changes, even ones we couldn't imagine before seeing it.

Design Intuition Takes Over: Honing the Art
SECTION II

Radical Landscape Change – Severe Site Changes

Design Intuition Takes Over: Honing the Art
SECTION II

Respecting the Existing Site

This backyard in Palo Alto, CA had this big mature Oak. Then the stage was added. The owners chose to keep the Oak and we lit it to blend in as part of the scene. To keep the stage the star, even when not in use, we lit only some of the Oak showing its form.

We let its top and ends fade into the dark night sky, and used downlights, which were turned off during performances, to create patterns on the back wall.

Design Intuition Takes Over: Honing the Art
SECTION II

Respecting the Existing Site

Over the course of a career, you get to experience big challenges. Arriving at this Vermont home, we looked out the living room window and saw lawn, some trees, and a fence. While the trees were outside the fence, it didn't dawn on us why the fence was placed that way, until we took a walk.

In the upper right photo, you can see that Michael Myer and Peping Dee are surprised, wondering how to light an abandoned quarry. Growing up in Connecticut, our swimming holes were called 'the quarries', and I learned why. Up the hill from here was another quarry that had completely filled up with water, rendering it useless. As that water seeped through these lower walls, removing the Vermont stone was stopped at this quarry too.

The upper right photo shows the wall's edge where all of us are standing. At right, you can see some water still seeping through the walls at the back intersection of left and right walls.

I contemplated how to light an abandoned quarry in someone's back yard .

Design Intuition Takes Over: Honing the Art
SECTION II
Respecting the Existing Site

We chose to wait until late winter to do a mockup, both for our information and to show the clients how the quarry could look if lit. We had hoped that the seeping water would look like it does here; over the winter months forming these big, long icicles. At that back intersection of walls, look at the aqua color, also showing in the ends of some of the big icicles: the natural color of the water coming through the stone.

Design Intuition Takes Over: Honing the Art
SECTION II
Respecting the Existing Site

Using snowshoes to reach the quarry in February 2003, Tom Williams and I brought a few fixtures, both metal halide and halogen MR16 low voltage fixtures, with multiple extension cords. At the right end of the quarry, we stepped out on a ledge and placed the fixtures with the results you see on both these pages.

We used the metal halide fixtures to make sure we captured that aqua ice color. We placed them at a grazing angle to get that glint reflecting off as many ice icicles as possible. We wanted to make sure that the roughly four foot high cuts the stone masons made as they had worked their way down into the earth showed as well as at night as they do during the day.

We hoped that the view from inside the toasty warm house would entice the owners and guests to make their own trek on snow shoes out to the north edge of the quarry, to see that amazing view down into the hole, whether winter or summer.

This is certainly a different kind of, "existing", site. This planet earth has many interesting places to share with us whose beauty could be appreciated after dark.

Design Intuition Takes Over: Honing the Art
SECTION II
Respecting the Existing Site

Called to come to one of the remote islands along the coast of Maine, I found myself in this cloudy, foggy forest wonderland. I had just completed the owners' South Carolina home, preparing for the walking cocktail parties, so they knew what I could do in the landscape. Here, as I often did, I designed the interior lighting as well as the landscape lighting. That gave me the insight into how the two would work together at this home.

On my first visit I stayed multiple days at a local hotel in town. The house was under construction, so we could walk through and review the design we had agreed on. The main purpose of the visit was to get a sense of place and how the buildings fit into the site. While the wife agreed the SC landscape lighting was intriguing and she loved it, she still wanted the lighting here to be understated.

Design Intuition Takes Over: Honing the Art
SECTION II
Respecting the Existing Site

Using mostly downlighting along the face of the home's front, with a little uplighting on the big stone fireplace wall, I used the warmth of the interior lighting and the two big nautical lanterns as an aid to draw your eye to the front door. Of course, a high light level on the front porch helped. With light reflecting off the walls, the owners agreed that no path lighting was necessary. You can still clearly see the walk at this front end of the house, while most friends would be arriving by boat at the dock, at the back side of the house.

Looking more closely, you can see the eave mounted downlights that light the very newly planted garden beds along the home's walls. This back lit the columns for the most part, with a little light spilling onto their bases and the stone pedestals – enough to show their architectural strength without drawing too much attention to them. Even without lighting trees behind this house, the architecture shows enough while the lighting remains understated.

Design Intuition Takes Over: Honing the Art
SECTION II
Respecting the Existing Site

The buildings wrap around a cove, so much of the back was right on the water at Burnt Cove. The house has many windows with amazing views. The lighting needed to continue providing views after dark. The owners chose to change the land as little as possible and keep the views limited to close to the buildings.

One important view is the lone tree on the rocks along the shore, seen in the photo above. Part of a larger scene, this mini-composition consisted of two fixtures mounted behind the shrub and aimed to reveal the stone and tree.

One challenge was to see if we could light some of the shore from a hidden area behind stones, without it affecting the Cove or arriving boats. We kept aiming the fixture down until the buoy just off shore was no longer visible. The owners confirmed the fixture wasn't visible by agreeing to go out in their boat and check.

Design Intuition Takes Over: Honing the Art
SECTION II
Respecting the Existing Site

This daytime photo shows the amazing rock formations and the trees coming right up out of the stones. Surrounded by the cove and a bay, this property didn't get big wave action from storms. Nonetheless, we worked hard to locate fixtures where they would not be seen or interfere with beach life and would last in this difficult environment.

Another view shows that we lit along the beach to provide a way to sit down and enjoy the waves lapping along the shore in the evening. One fixture attached to the wall does that grazing at left. Another expands the view of the rock formations with the little tree and other locations to the left of the tree including the area connecting it to the conifers at the top of the hill. The view of the evergreen trees was primarily from the house, but I wanted some continuity on the back side as seen from the sitting beach.

Design Intuition Takes Over: Honing the Art
SECTION II
Respecting the Existing Site

Construction was taking place when I took this first photo of that copse of trees. The temporary fencing shows how close the trees are to the house. Beyond them you can see how close they are to the water as well.

This existing wall provided the perfect mounting location for the uplighting of these trees. We are all making notes on how to get power here, how many fixtures will be located, where to light the fronts of these trees for the view from inside the house and from the adjacent patio (which you can almost see on the right).

Design Intuition Takes Over: Honing the Art
SECTION II
Respecting the Existing Site

The wall was high enough to mount canopies low on the wall with the glare shields barely showing above the wall. If you look closely you can see about half an inch of the glare shield – look for a little fog at the shield.

The downlighting around the house allowed people to move down the stairs to the lawn level and walk out to the beach.

Design Intuition Takes Over: Honing the Art
SECTION II

Snow's Effect on Landscape Lighting

Even though the view is nothing special, looking out this living room window, with the snow on the Azalea shrub's leaves and light in the woods, it feels as if you're connected, without getting cold or wet.

This is the view from my sleeping porch in Upstate NY where I lived for nearly 20 years. Having that view from my bathroom tub was a wonderful joy. Every night it was dark unless ILLI (see page 326) was conducting a class, and then it was amazing for a couple of nights.

This little Maple was a demonstration tree just outside my office. We lit it as a young tree, as you see here with downlight and uplight. The snow gives it such character, and the shadows on the snow from the downlight add the magic.

Nothing though, is as amazing as seeing this same view covered by the bounty of snow. It is like fairy land, and when you add light to that, there is just nothing better.

Design Intuition Takes Over: Honing the Art
SECTION II

Snow's Effect on Landscape Lighting

Looking out this Lake Tahoe cabin window in the summer is wonderful, but snow on the ground adds depth to the scene.

This is looking along a stream behind the cabin during the day, summer night, and winter night. It seems amazing to me how different each scene looks, even though I know it is the same. The snow adds another dimension to reality and gives us another world to inhabit for a few nights or, if lucky, a few months.

Design Intuition Takes Over: Honing the Art
SECTION II

Snow's Effect on Landscape Lighting

Summer night out my dining room window in Upstate New York. I had waited years to see the Maple.

In the mid-fall, the Maple steals the scene with its changing bright red colors.

Then in the winter the Maple takes a back seat, and the snow blanket just demands your attention. But the snow cover is always fleeting. I loved being able to admire it from inside most nights because it was lit. Lighting erases the black mirrors that windows become at night and gives us art.

Design Intuition Takes Over: Honing the Art
SECTION II

Snow's Effect on Landscape Lighting

In some locations, snow pack of varying height stays for the whole winter so we have to plan how to still welcome guests yet allow them to move around.

Night takes away a lot of our sense of surroundings, so we have to decide what to give ourselves back for safety and aesthetics.

Here, Lighting Research Center (LRC) students have put ring-mount fixtures in the trees to light the shoveled path. They also uplit trees along the way to increase our sense of space, and moved a water feature to the end of the path to provide a visual destination.

This forest edge was seen from the back of my Upstate NY home. Over the 18 years it changed quite a bit as I developed the gardens.

Early on, an LRC student design team lit that forest as a spectacular view from the house, using primarily metal halide, with a little incandescent to show depth into the forest.

Design Intuition Takes Over: Honing the Art
SECTION II

Snow's Effect on Landscape Lighting

LRC students helped me study the effect of snow on lighting in garden spaces. A 2000 design team was the first to play with light on this Acer platinoides/Norway Maple tree. In *The Landscape Lighting Book*, third Edition, I show the lighting effects over the course of a year through all the seasons on this tree, but snow gives it the most dazzling effect in the dark.

The evergreen trees behind it with no light still show because of the snow blanketing their branches.

We had one night to get this lighting right. It happened in very late winter and the snow was gone by the end of the next day. Everyone dropped what they were doing that Sunday and we spent the night getting photos throughout all the areas this class lit.

Design Intuition Takes Over: Honing the Art
SECTION II

Snow's Effect on Landscape Lighting

This view of the back of my Upstate NY home shows three Juglans nigra/Black Walnut trees. Nearly 100 years old, they tower over the house. Two of them flank one set of the stairs to the back kitchen entry.

Lit in the summer, they are majestic and give us a view from the screened sleeping porch; a wonderful view to enjoy. Their downlighting makes a clear path down those stairs out to the rest of the property.

Winter in Upstate NY is long and hard. Having snow clinging to the branches in these trees and on top of the shrubs at the top of the stairs is a wonderful momentary experience. Once again, you can see how much more light downlights can cover when mounted in a tree, and, how that expands and opens up the space in the winter.

Design Intuition Takes Over: Honing the Art
SECTION II

Snow's Effect on Landscape Lighting

This Morus alba/White Mulberry tree has a wispy vase-shape with dense branching and dense leaf overlap making it difficult to get light through the canopy in the summer time. I used to have to prune its weeping branches as I kept hitting my head while mowing the yard.

With those horizontal, weeping branches, it holds snow during and just after a snow storm. Its branches are strong, unlike some of the conifers whose branches would break from top to bottom due to the weight of the snow. When a top branch breaks from the weight, it takes all the rest below off with it.

In 1999 an LRC student design team lit this tree for the first time. They lit is as a view from the picnic bench using three fixtures, all located in front of the tree. That makes it look two-dimensional.

They located one of the three fixtures under the canopy to light the trunk, visually tying the canopy to the ground. It's a little too close to the front trunk, making a hot spot. With a little night aiming, they could move it or re-aim it to avoid that – the finesse that makes all the difference comes during aiming.

A few years later, another LRC student lit the tree again. Without showing the previous student's work, before they lit their chosen subject, Michael Myer located and aimed the trunk fixture to still show the multi-trunk form, and softer than the previous effort. All the lighting is softer. Using less brightness is something we all learned as we keep working over the years. While it doesn't take much brightness, it usually takes multiple fixtures to show three dimensional form, details, and texture.

Design Intuition Takes Over: Honing the Art
SECTION II
Snow's Effect on Landscape Lighting

Whenever I discuss winter lighting, the question of how much snow can fall before uplighting doesn't work, comes up. A good question. I first studied it working in Lake Tahoe, where the snow pack – the height of snow that stays on the ground all winter – could be 4'/1.2m or more. Continuing to research it over time in NY, I learned that halogen in-grade fixtures can burn off up to 3'/1m of snow on top of a fixture, aimed straight up. During a big snowstorm, I suggest turning your lighting on to allow the lamps/fixtures, whether in-grade or stake mount halogen or LED to melt the snow as it falls. No matter what, the fixtures melt snow in big circles around them.

Once we started changing lamps to LED and installing integral module LED fixtures, we found that while we think of LED as 'not producing heat', they actually just produce less heat than old technology lamps. Whether in-grade or stake-mount with replacement lamps or integral modules, it takes a couple days longer, but as you see in the two photos above at the top, both types of fixtures and lamps do melt the snow, just like the neon bone does on page 98.

If a fixture is aimed too much off zenith (straight up), then it becomes nearly impossible to melt enough snow. In the lower left photo, you can see that I have shoveled snow off the top of a fixture aimed down from 0° to nearly 90° to light the trunks of a distant tree. I have shoveled out snow from the ground to just over the fixture's top to show the depth of that snow from that storm. At right, I measured the depth of snow being melted by that LED fixture.

Design Intuition Takes Over: Honing the Art
SECTION II

Snow's Effect on Landscape Lighting

It may be obvious that I love lighting trees. This is an Oak at David Brearey's' home – our ILLI pruning expert. He has lit acres of his property in Maine for people to come visit during all seasons (hillroadlighting.com).

This is a Quercus alba/White Oak by his house. He has lit straight up by the trunk through the canopy. In all the snow they accumulate in Maine, he keeps the view of that tree working most of the winter.

Design Intuition Takes Over: Honing the Art
SECTION II

Renderings – Imagery to Assist Clients to Visualize Your Ideas

When I met George, his artistic talent and photography expertise worked together as he started making project renderings for me. Either he or I would take a photo – he wants high resolution in RAW format. I would describe how I would light the scene – up, down, or combination, and the hierarchy of brightnesses. Working with George was not the first time I used renderings. Trooper Dan Dyer, NY State, worked for me while waiting to qualify for the entrance exam to become a trooper (he has architecture and lighting degrees from RPI). He produced one for our Chicago Botanic Gardens conceptual design presentation. But with George, I learned I could email a client thousands of miles away and we could discuss the lighting before they got very far into the project.

The rendering above is a plan showing the scope of the lighting for this Bahamas home. George used the 'values key' to express the brightness variation and color to show which trees would be uplit. The tannish-yellow layer shows the downlighting.

While renderings may not be exactly realistic, the way George renders scenes looks so realistic sometimes it's hard to differentiate between the rendering and the actual lighting photo.

This allowed me to now email ideas to a client to show conceptual ideas, a new thought, or multiple options. The distance between them, the site, and me diminished with this skill.

Design Intuition Takes Over: Honing the Art
SECTION II
Renderings – Imagery to Assist Clients to Visualize Your Ideas

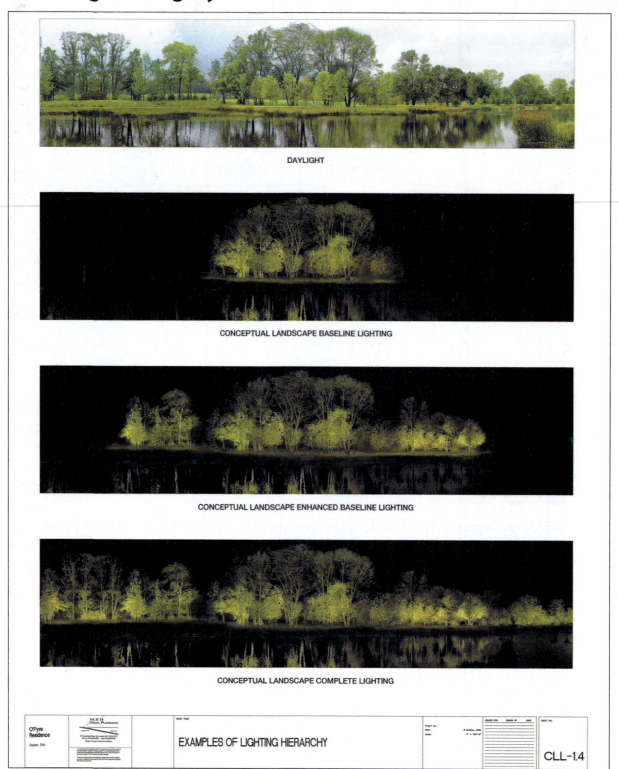

This was the first rendering George did for me – the view across the lake from the boat house in Ohio. The architects wanted to give the client options for scope and hoped that they would approve the 'Enhanced Baseline" option. They presented my ideas and called to advise me that the clients had requested the 'complete' scenario. Our only restriction was to not use a quantity of more than one thousand 1000 watt transformers: a control system limitation. We didn't use nearly that many.

Design Intuition Takes Over: Honing the Art
SECTION II

Renderings – Imagery to Assist Clients to Visualize Your Ideas

This photo shows the boat house under construction, and, its view.

George's rendering shows how the view could look. He didn't 'finish' the boat house.

This is a photograph of the final lighting. It's not exactly the same, but very close. In the beginning we didn't know about that back line of conifers behind the existing trees. In the photo, the reflection is much stronger than in George's rendering. He says he has learned a lot since doing that series of renderings.

Design Intuition Takes Over: Honing the Art
SECTION II
Renderings – Imagery to Assist Clients to Visualize Your Ideas

This is a rendering of a parking area where the owners stored their trash cans. It was also a view from their back garden patio. The rendering keeps light away from the trash cans and reveals the elephant sculpture just above and beyond the cans, which you have to search for in the daytime photo. George's process starts with a high quality camera for the daytime imagery. He then does all the rendering with hundreds of layers in Photoshop. It is time consuming, but can be updated easily and is very transportable.

Design Intuition Takes Over: Honing the Art
SECTION II

Renderings – Imagery to Assist Clients to Visualize Your Ideas

In Villanova, PA I arrived in the car you see in this daytime photo. I asked the client to stop the car. We needed to discuss the feeling of this space and what lighting could do to continue that experience after dark. This was the only photo I had taken of the allée during my initial visit. It had to work. George made it work, even showing reflections off the car.

I wanted the client to see that I would limit the lighting to the 'inside' of this allée. I would concentrate light in the upper canopy to visually support the daytime 'uplifting' feeling you get when you are standing in the allée.

It was important to show that the outer edge of the canopy on the owners' house side, toward us in the rendering, would remain dark, as well as the other sides of the allée. This is for the simple physical reason that the parking area expands both left and right at this end of the trees, limiting our fixture location.

While I could have put below-grade fixtures in the ground at the parking area, I preferred not to, as the shadowing at the house end continues the experience of containing the light within the allée.

Compare this daytime shot and the rendering with the photos of the allée over time, pages 33 and 76–78. Again, not exactly the same, and the lighting changes over the years as the allée matures, but this captures the conceptual idea. The owners loved the concept and cherish the lit allée.

Design Intuition Takes Over: Honing the Art
SECTION II

Renderings – Imagery to Assist Clients to Visualize Your Ideas

Some people want to go deep in the forest to get away from the hubbub of their day to day life; in this case, a beautiful deciduous forest leading to a get away home. The family liked to walk the dirt entry drive and the paths through their Upstate NY property. We discussed only downlighting along the drive and into the forest to keep their privacy intact. This was an early rendering to help them understand the overall site approach. Near or around the house, even the gardens hadn't yet been developed, so we waited to introduce ideas near the house.

Design Intuition Takes Over: Honing the Art
SECTION II

Renderings – Imagery to Assist Clients to Visualize Your Ideas

At this Colorado property, the owners had created interesting experiences along a long drive that cut all the way through the property. Looking at the space, I suggested we use the big tree along side the left of the creek to downlight the bridge and its railings that have lots of symbolism. A little light around the upcoming corner would show you the next surprise, shown on page 177.

Design Intuition Takes Over: Honing the Art
SECTION II

Renderings – Imagery to Assist Clients to Visualize Your Ideas

This owner had not realized that his house could be seen from the gate until we presented this rendering. We introduced the gates, used the allée of trees to frame the view to the house, and used a cooler color on the evergreens for contrast to visually reveal the house up the hill – with the highest light level on the trees surrounding the house.

Design Intuition Takes Over: Honing the Art
SECTION II

Renderings – Imagery to Assist Clients to Visualize Your Ideas

Some renderings require a lot of cleaning up. Here, George finished the entry patio ground cover, filled in the yet to be planted hedges, added the trees on both sides of the entry door, removed the red truck – he even installed the correct path lights with all the lighting that I was suggesting. His technique keeps evolving, as everyone's art does as they tackle new ideas or situations. He carefully leaves part of the home dark, but doesn't erase it completely, as the reflections in this entry space would reveal them slightly and allow me to draw your attention to the front door.

Design Intuition Takes Over: Honing the Art
SECTION II

Renderings – Imagery to Assist Clients to Visualize Your Ideas

This series is the one I refer to most regarding how effective renderings can be for designers. I gave George the daytime photo and he diligently put in the downlighting over the planting along the walk. That big branch above your head he shows with a little bit of reflection. Sending this image off to the owners, they said 'OH. I see why you suggested uplighting the Oaks in the front '. They thought uplighting wouldn't be necessary as they wanted to keep the front dark.

Design Intuition Takes Over: Honing the Art
SECTION II

Renderings – Imagery to Assist Clients to Visualize Your Ideas

This property is in Northern CA, and I had lived in NY for nearly a decade by then. Being able to email ideas like this back and forth helped us determine the scope and conceptual design without another trip to the West Coast at that point. In the photo on the right, you can see I didn't have enough uplight for the trees on either side of the front porch in the rendering. You can catch things like that, otherwise easily overlooked.

That final lighting photo, at right, shows the similarity of the rendering to the real lighting. They replaced the ground cover planting with new plants before we finished the lighting installation, but with a smaller species than the plants in the rendering. This opens up the space using less shrubs and more ground cover.

The big difference in the lighting you can see in the photo – the big branches and trunk now show. Below, the photo shows the wonder created by uplighting the Oak canopies. The walk would not have shown people how amazing mature California Live Oak trees are without that uplighting. That canopy is perhaps the best part of the lighting scene.

Design Intuition Takes Over: Honing the Art
SECTION II

Renderings – Imagery to Assist Clients to Visualize Your Ideas

Los Angeles lighting designer Sean O'Conner (seanocconerlighting.com), asked George to prepare this rendering of this vast open space at a project in Montecito that I had helped him figure out how to light. The client wasn't there much and wanted to see Sean's ideas. Keeping the space private and quiet was an important need for the project.

Design Intuition Takes Over: Honing the Art
SECTION II

Renderings – Imagery to Assist Clients to Visualize Your Ideas

The 2016 ILLI intensive course in Ridgewood, NJ, had started as an in-house project. My then partner Brooke Silber and I decided to have it become a permanent installation through an ILLI Intensive Course.

The rendering was done while it was the company project. The ILLI design team who then worked on that area had to be true to the rendering.

The American Eagle atop this memorial statue had to be the focal point. Uplighting wouldn't work due to the size of the plinth under the bird.

There are big trees not visible in the photos that the team used to light the eagle, from both sides. They also downlight several details, including the memorial plaque of names; very critical to this monument. The downlighting spills onto the walkways around the monument.

While I normally want your eye to be visually brought back to the ground, this was a time to break the rule.

175

Design Intuition Takes Over: Honing the Art
SECTION II

Renderings – Imagery to Assist Clients to Visualize Your Ideas

Sometimes amazing parts of a client's property are mostly not noticed until they receive a rendering. This stream, like many in Upstate NY, has water certain times of the year. The owner didn't notice how beautiful the stream and its surroundings actually were because it spent most of the year as a dry stream.

As the rendering suggests, all the lighting for this scene would be downlighting. While I normally start my thinking with downlighting, sometimes I end up with only downlighting as it uses so few fixtures to cover the entire scene. The lighting effects last much longer and it keeps the scene visually soft and quiet.

Design Intuition Takes Over: Honing the Art
SECTION II

Renderings – Imagery to Assist Clients to Visualize Your Ideas

Back at the Colorado roadway we first looked at in the rendering on page 169, this area has a surprise. Looking at this photo and rendering, you might think it is the horse sculptures arriving, but it actually is the scene carved into that branch stub at the lower right in both the photo and rendering. Then it continues with the horses and more surprises along further along the way.

You could say that the magic of the carving, and having it lit, is drawing the horses up and out from the field.

Design Intuition Takes Over: Honing the Art
SECTION II

Shadows Define Space– Providing Emphasis or Finesse

Shadows are an important design tool helping us to understand form. Without shadows everything looks flat. Shadows can be over, under, and/or between parts of a plant, on the trunk of a tree, on a sculpture, just under the top of a wall or cascading down a wall; both of those from above.

We can use shadows to reveal or to hide things in a scene. However, too much darkness or shadow can become uncomfortable.

Shadow is one tool in our box. We have to plan and then manipulate light for shadows to produce the lighting effects we want in our compositions.

Design Intuition Takes Over: Honing the Art
SECTION II

Shadows Define Space – Providing Emphasis or Finesse

Along a walk to Evening Island at CBG, I am using big darkness, between the Salix babylonica/Weeping Willows on both sides of the bridge and the carillon, as a tool to ensure that you don't miss the tower: the focal point on the island. I have discussed uplighting from under the tower's bells, and how the shadows made there help define the detail of the mechanisms creating the bell tones.

Uplighting the Willlows, I introduced shadows on the trunks by grazing the bark to show texture, with the trunk lit more brightly, grounding the tree. I lit the canopies unevenly, using shadow to show the size and form of the canopy as well as the leaf structure in the canopy.

We can use darkness to reveal form, and to hide elements we don't want revealed as they would diminish the effectiveness or beauty of the scene we are creating. We can use shadows to complete a form by lighting throughout a canopy but leaving some areas unlit. Sometimes I leave part of a canopy dark to emphasize the focal point in a scene, (see page 217). Shadows can emphasize texture on evergreen boughs and architectural surfaces. They can make plain surfaces, walls, floors, lawns, more interesting.

Darkness between areas can be the element that creates the tension or separates elements. Shadows can fill large expanses to provide visual connection or they can keep a site visually quiet by showing some paving with soft patterning. Think about using them in most, if not all your projects.

Design Intuition Takes Over: Honing the Art
SECTION II

Shadows Define Space – Providing Emphasis or Finesse

In the Connecticut project, upper left, the big tree is lit only from the front, so the form appears two-dimensional and the downlight on the structure's roof shows form, texture, and detail.

This Fagus grandiflora/American Beech, above, has multiple fixtures for this mock up that would be below-grade fixtures in an actual installation. Look at the variation in brightness across that canopy with even a little bit reaching the inset highest branch. In an ILLI Intensive Course class, Don Bradley used a series of downlights to show the multiple trunks softly connecting with the canopy.

Design Intuition Takes Over: Honing the Art
SECTION II

Shadows Define Space – Providing Emphasis or Finesse

Downlighting from the inside of a multi-trunk tree shows the trunks best. In the upper left photo, the variation is brightness within the canopy and with the branches stronger than in the photo at right. The lower photo has a tiny amount of brightness variation in the canopy and more along the walkways, with stronger light showing where the offshoot walks lead. The location and project conditions determine how much light to use.

Design Intuition Takes Over: Honing the Art
SECTION II

Shadows Define Space – Providing Emphasis or Finesse

For the two trees in Pennsylvania at top, the back tree has uplights for the trunk/branching structure, while the right tree adds tree-mounted downlights, making it much softer and showing the ground plane. In Connecticut in the 1990s, above, halogen below-grade fixtures light the Apple trees much brighter, just off the back patio. The whole scene is brighter. Now my lighting has become much softer, easier to live with.

Design Intuition Takes Over: Honing the Art
SECTION II

Shadows Define Space – Providing Emphasis or Finesse

Similar comparison here. Connecticut in the 1990s at top and Long Island, NY below. The uplighting shows the texture in both. At top, a much stronger statement and below a softer one.

Design Intuition Takes Over: Honing the Art
SECTION II

Shadows Define Space – Providing Emphasis or Finesse

This kitchen garden in Upstate NY, has lighting under a very old low clipped hedge to show its branching structure. Using bright light there provides general lighting at the picnic table area and balances with the bollard, also providing general area light and announcing the back entry. Notice the bollard has one of our Salukis running as the pattern.

Design Intuition Takes Over: Honing the Art
SECTION II

Shadows Define Space – Providing Emphasis or Finesse

The tree photos, at left and on this page use downlighting to fill in the ground plane. At lower left is a Beachside framing projector (beachsidelighting.com), with a gobo pattern of branches. At top, shining a light down through branches creates patterns on the paving, some in focus, others not. At bottom, the downlighting introduces some ground plane as fill along the drive approaching this home at the top of a long driveway up a long hill.

Design Intuition Takes Over: Honing the Art
SECTION II

Shadows Define Space – Providing Emphasis or Finesse

Here, downlighting in the Oak trees reveals this remote wall to introduce depth from the arrival courtyard of this Napa, CA project. It also lights the ground plane and shrubbery in front of the wall, providing context. The Oaks are uplit. Lighting the ground plane, trees, and wall completes a scene. This mini-scene aids guests as well as the maintenance staff going back to their cars at night. Providing well-conceived mini-compositions in the distance helps reveal large space and gives continuity to the overall property lighting design.

Design Intuition Takes Over: Honing the Art
SECTION II

Shadows Define Space – Providing Emphasis or Finesse

At this Atherton, CA indoor pool, the owner collects and paints palm trees (see palmpaintings.com). She and her husband like to swim every night. Edith asked if I could light the palms so that she can see them around her while swimming. I told her I could do that and create shadow patterns at the pool edges and on the pool deck in addition to lighting the palms. She loved that idea.

The downlights are positioned and aimed so that swimming either direction, the pair have no glare whether doing the crawl or backstroke.

Design Intuition Takes Over: Honing the Art
SECTION II

Shadows Define Space – Providing Emphasis or Finesse

Down the street from my home in Upstate NY, the owner of this carefully tended garden wanted a view from their pool patio. With budget limitations, we chose to light one remote tree at the edge of the forest and concentrate on the area closest to the pool. Notice that the garden uplighting softly reveals the big trees behind the garden at the edge of the woods.

Not Just Another Light Source
Disruptive Technology Causes New Learning
My Client Bought the Property Next Door

A light source, the lamp or 'bulb' as it is often inaccurately called, is only one part of the the light fixture assembly that produces light. LED was introduced to humans long before it became viable to use architecturally, and, years after that, for it to be worthwhile in landscape lighting. It hit the market like a lightning strike. Everyone, their brother, and even their dog, thought that they could sell LED, not having solved problems like limiting the heat at the positive/negative junction point or attempting to prevent a minuscule amount of moisture infiltrating the fixture cavity from forming enough corrosion to cause LEDs to fail. Once the challenges were resolved, LED took off like wildfire. As my husband George always notes, horses weren't banned with the advent of automobiles, but California has banned incandescent light sources.

Today, 2021, I haven't used halogen (incandescent) sources for about seven years. Why? LED offers us low wattages – less than 0.5 watts to 7.5 – compared to up to 75 watts of halogen used in the 1990s. They are more efficient, but, the main reason to use them is that we can reduce total wattage consumption by 70–80% on every project. Long life is still not a proven reality.

I designed this project for a long term client in the SF Bay Area, originally in the mid 1980's. They purchased the next door property when the owner died. That piece of land had originally been part of the parcel and was split off before my clients purchased the property. That split made their backyard narrow with a long, very remote and private dog-leg. Now the backyard is a big rectangle, making it appear much larger, more visible to the owners and more useful for them. For lighting, it meant starting over.

The Man with Bird sculpture moved from a distant vista, (see pages 24–27 & 101) to becoming the star at the main patio. Much of the lighting at the patio remained the same, but, I added a downlight in the Jacaranda tree to light the top of the sculpture's hat. For the rest of the space, everything was new, but, several sculptures were relocated and became easier to see and enjoy.

Not Just Another Light Source *Disruptive Technology Causes New Learning*
SECTION III
My Client Bought the Property Next Door

Now the project is completely LED; a combination of integral module, with individual fixture output dimming (before the control system) and flexible beam distribution by HK Lighting Group, (hklightinggroup.com) and simple LED retrofit lamps. The stone sculpture, previously directly across from the home's doors, has moved into the new rose garden on the left, as you stand on the patio. The previous lighting, lower right, was only uplighting from two stake mount adjustable fixtures. Now, lower left, you see the texture of the stone and depth through back uplighting, with both stake mount LED uplights and downlights mounted in the palm trees behind the sculpture.

In the previous garden, the two palm trees were inconspicuous. Here they frame the sculpture. Uplighting grazes the hedge along the edge of the garden, as it did in the original garden. The rose frames have below grade fixture inside each one providing three-dimensional light on the climbing roses. Downlights integrated into the curved entry arch, with the climbing roses quickly growing up the structure quickly, show the entry to this garden space.

Disruptive Technology Causes New Learning **Not Just Another Light Source**
SECTION III

My Client Bought the Property Next Door

Above, ring mount fixtures in the structure covered now with grape vines shows the entry and stairs to the vegetable garden. The cat sculpture, mostly hidden in the old gardens, now greets you. The eating pavilion, lower, has moved to one end of the new garden by the barbecue center built into the back of the garage (left yellow wall). MR11 adjustable downlights are built into the outer trellis members for plants surrounding, and inside for the table and serving area, with a sculpture on the counter, of course. Changing the project from halogen to LED always causes the plant material to appear more vivid.

Not Just Another Light Source *Disruptive Technology Causes New Learning*
SECTION III

Historic Property Gets Sculpture

The 1930's historic Long Island Goodyear home was saved by a New York developer. Entering the property, (lower image), trees on either side are softly lit uplit with downlighting introducing the two pad drive. Resting on a rise, the modern Edward Durell Stone structure beckons you. In the upper photo at right, you see the towering female sculpture surrounded by the grove of trees uplit with below grade fixtures and downlights softly showing the ground plane. Trees framing the dining room, with canopies pruned to show the architectural shape, have below grade uplights and tree mount adjustable downlights casting the shadows on the two wing walls. The large, distant tree, beyond the pool visually ties the structure with the art field, at right. This is the first, of many, projects with David Kelly of Rees Roberts + Partners Landscape, (reesroberts.com).

Disruptive Technology Causes New Learning   **Not Just Another Light Source**
SECTION III

Historic Property Gets Sculpture

The upper photo shows the shadow patterns created by aiming through the tree canopies, necessary, as we had to limit the location of the below grade uplights and, as you see, the canopies extend toward the roof. Finding locations to light through the canopy to create those shadows is a tool I have used since my CA home, (page 14). Along the right wall, is a water runnel with light spilling onto it and the stairs. At left, an original brick wall with openings surrounds the kitchen garden, and we lit the inner surface to create the patterning on the 'public' side. As usual, I let the light fade to show the curve in the wall, while highlighting the end and the left wing wall to quietly show the private walkway.

Not Just Another Light Source *Disruptive Technology Causes New Learning*
SECTION III

Historic Property Gets Sculpture

Not all the artwork we are asked to light, we fall in love with, yet we do the best we can to show it at night. This very large Hello Kitty, with two soft uplights located to show her in three dimensions and one uplight to fill in behind her, watches the end of the pool, with the riot of trees forming a background beyond the pool. The 'green wall' of both evergreen and deciduous trees lined the entire property using three transformers and dozens of uplights set at different distances and with varying wattage and beam spread.

Back at the dining room patio space, you see the patterning on the runnel wall with the below grade lights all contained under the tree canopies, away from the patio space. Using the downlights to aim through the outer canopy allows the group to be seen from the dining room and along the entry drive.

In the distance you have a glimpse of that very tall sculpture of a pregnant woman, with her skin removed on one side, between the last two trees in the distance. Honoring the owners art choice, we lit her, but softly so the very graphic demonstration of our human body is downplayed from this viewing point.

Disruptive Technology Causes New Learning **Not Just Another Light Source**

Clients Keep Changing Their Art

I lit this Westchester County project originally at least ten years earlier (see pages 79–82). The client called Brooke Silber, my partner, at the time, for some new art to be lit. He had added these very severe modern sculptures on the 'upper lawn' viewed from the house. The forest behind the art, I had included in the original design, but it wasn't installed at that time. Brooke, convinced him that without lighting the forest, the sculptures would lack context.

She varied the up and downlighting on the trees throughout the forest to frame the art. To show the severe shape, she lit the pieces from the corners; a technique I have used for architectural structure, art pieces, and furniture over the years. If these had been washed, rather than grazing the corners, the lighting effect would be less striking.

Not Just Another Light Source *Disruptive Technology Causes New Learning*
SECTION III

A Very Quiet Place

Working again with David Kelly of Rees Roberts in Southampton, NY, this client urged extreme lighting constraint. Looking at the model, at the start of the project, we suggested edge lighting the plantings ringing the pond that wrap around the back of the property and the pool. Using my shore-scraping technique, originally developed for the Chicago Botanic Garden, (pages 103) and in Ohio (pages106–107) with lights placed behind the water plants on the house side, and on the 'front' or pond-side for the far boundary. As with other projects, the fixtures are wet-dry and located in the water. The transformers are remotely located up the hill, outside the water flood line.

Disruptive Technology Causes New Learning **Not Just Another Light Source**
SECTION III

A Very Quiet Place

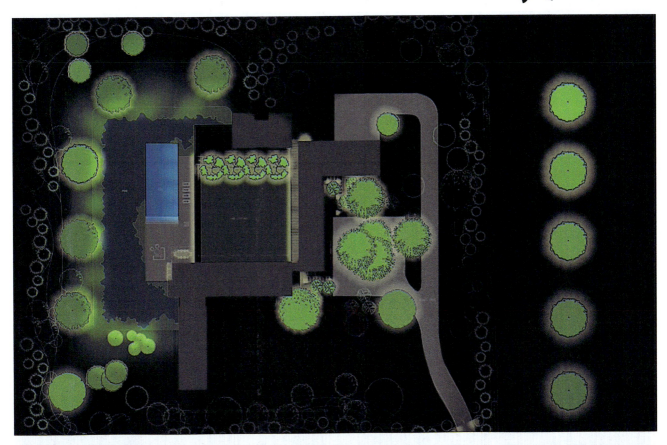

The original design rendering shows lighting on the trees beyond the pond's far edge, but, they have not been lit, as yet. At the arrival, a central drive tree provides soft downlighting to show the entry area. Very soft uplighting of the trees provides vertical lighting to complete the scene's composition. The sculpture is lit to draw attention toward the front door with completely shielded copper path lights (matching materials with the pathlights) from Escort Lighting, (escortlighting.com), very gently lighting the stairs, but remaining understated both day and night.

Not Just Another Light Source *Disruptive Technology Causes New Learning*
SECTION III

A Very Quiet Place

Looking across the pool/pond, you can barely see the outline of the trees' beyond. Not lighting them keeps the space very quiet in the neighborhood. The lower photo shows the effect of allowing light to wash the front of the trees, just outside the master bedroom windows. By only lighting the front, and, with fixtures located at ground level, the tree backsides remain dark, and the ground plane plantings hide the fixtures from view outside the property.

Lower right, you see the other side of the entry drive (see page 197). We continued the technique of downlighting the planting around the entry courtyard with downlighting through the trees' canopies, creating shadow patterns on the ground throughout the area. People not only function well with the boundaries being lit and some information of the ground on which they travel, but, with these patterns, they really enjoy the experience.

Disruptive Technology Causes New Learning   **Not Just Another Light Source**
SECTION III

A Very Quiet Place

A hedge separates the inner courtyard from the pond area (upper photo) with the shore-scraping showing just over the hedge to show your destination at the end of this walk. We uplit the row of pathway trees, helping people understand their movement through the space. Downlighting through the canopy casts shadows on the paving, and onto the gate, gently identifying the way.

Not Just Another Light Source *Disruptive Technology Causes New Learning*
SECTION III
Even More Quiet

Disruptive Technology Causes New Learning   **Not Just Another Light Source**
SECTION III

Even More Quiet

Back in Westchester County, NY on a large parcel of land, we needed to keep this property very understated for the clients. We lit the big trees quite a way along the entry drive to start introducing arrival. We showed the massive form of some trees, and/or the branching structure with uplighting, while continuing to visually connect the scene to the ground with tree mounted downlighting.

In several remote areas we reveal the gardens. Above, the runnel comes down through the planting levels and into and through the secret garden water feature. The ground plane has downlighting from another of the big, mature trees with light coming through the canopies; enough to show the water feature's shape and create the sense of a ceiling plane.

By this time, fully engrossed in using integral module LED with output tuning (dimming at the fixture, before the control system) and flex-beam allowing the movement of the bezel to adjust the amount of beam spread width, we have accepted the crisper light color produced by LED and embrace the new flexibility LED offers in one fixture, so that we can more easily create the exact effects that we imagined in conceptual design. Giving up the warmth of halogen incandescence was not easy, but the benefits fixture manufacturers are able to offer us, make it worth it.

Not Just Another Light Source *Disruptive Technology Causes New Learning*
SECTION III
Even More Quiet

Disruptive Technology Causes New Learning   **Not Just Another Light Source**
SECTION III

Even More Quiet

At left, the massive tree above the stairs announces the way to the pool, lights the way in, and even with most of the lighting soft, we get that beautiful reflection in the pool's surface. Using that combination of uplighting with downlighting always makes the space more amazing.

The owner allowed us to raise the lighting level only around the back patio. We used fixtures located within the planting beds, which, of course, changes effect through the growing season: a more maintenance intense technique.

Not Just Another Light Source *Disruptive Technology Causes New Learning*
SECTION III
Living Along the Top Edge of a Canyon

On a hill in Northern CA, Garden Light LED's (GLL), (gardenlightled.com), owner Michelle Mueller worked with me and the property owner, using their equipment to give Pam amazing views through her gardens and windows at night. Walking down from her front gate to the hill's edge, you see the lights of the Bay Area beyond. GLL's color is vibrant supporting the magic space Pam has created for her very remote and private home. As you move to the entry, you constantly encounter the whimsy that explains Pam Morris's brilliance in designing beautiful lighting fixtures that are simply art.

Disruptive Technology Causes New Learning   **Not Just Another Light Source**
SECTION III

Living Along the Top Edge of a Canyon

Above, you see the masses of flowers that undulate along the front of the house, giving views here and privacy there which we enhance with light at night, giving Pam both intimate and Bay views. In her bedroom, she surrounds herself with bamboo to filter the Eastern morning light. She treasures that back lighting and for the night, we light the front of the bamboo, giving her a day/night contrast. We have stake mount uplights and roof mounted downlights creating this art to surround her sleep. In order for landscape lighting, even with the stronger output of LED to be viewed from indoors, the interior lighting needs to be much softer than the landscape lighting out the window.

Not Just Another Light Source *Disruptive Technology Causes New Learning*
SECTION III
Living Along the Top Edge of a Canyon

The backyard is a sitting area for relaxing in privacy. The patio is surrounded on two sides by the house; on one side by the jungle of planting that Pam keeps ever fuller, and the fourth side by a hillside with a massive tree. Pam is fascinated by the play of light and shadow and myriads of pattern.

Exciting Lighting Inc., Pam-Morris-Designs.com, pammorris@me.com, 415-846-6858
GardenLightLED.com, Michelle Mueller, michelle@gardenlightled.com, 813-901-5595

Disruptive Technology Causes New Learning **Not Just Another Light Source**
SECTION III

Living In the Sonoran Desert

George and I moved to the Sonoran Desert in 2015; I had waited since 1978. It is a different environment requiring rethinking, just as we have to marvel at how different the landscape looks when we see it for the first time. Not only is the landscape filled with rock and mountains; the remains of ancient Anazazi homes and multiple current-day American Indian tribes reservations; and plant material designed to protect itself from everything; for most of the year it begs us to live outdoors at night. Soft breezes and gently warm temperatures encourage outdoor living from September through June, until the summer heat and monsoon storms hit!

Yet, nothing really changes about design. We still need to provide a complete and cohesive visual composition with the different elements that comprise the landscape design.

At this project, the clients had some lighting, but, wanted to enhance the lighting effects. We added Excelsior Lighting, (excelsiorlighting.com), fixtures to this tree that they see out their bedroom window, taking advantage of the lower wattages available in LED replacement lamps. We used 5 watt, 60° beam spread, 3000°K lamps to show the overall form of the canopy. As you see, there is variation of brightness throughout the front side of the canopy to add three dimensional understanding. At the back left, you see that we chose to leave that backside dark out of respect for the neighbors. Notice the soft curve of the trunk and how it splits going front and back. Grazing by locating fixtures close to the trunk, clearly shows bark texture patterning. We did that with a tree-mounted downlight which visually ties the canopy to the ground and gives you more understanding of the beauty of the tree by highlighting the trunks shape and texture.

The tree is clearly the focal point. We have some ground light from an uplight whose purpose was the outside of the canopy, at left; we left the path light, in the middle; and have some downlight on the right plant providing the foreground with the deepening evening sky providing the background behind the tree.

Not Just Another Light Source *Disruptive Technology Causes New Learning*
SECTION III

Rio Verde Community Entrances

Rio Verde is a quiet community eight miles from the nearest town. It used to be WAY OUT WEST, but development encroaches. With multiple entrances, landscape lighting announces your arrival. At the top, the sign backlighting is 2700°K (the supplier wanted 6000°K which would NOT have worked) against the Corten steel panel. To that we added uplighting for the Palo Verde tree and Saguaro cactus, both Sonoran Desert natives, along with softly washing the stone column and grazing the stone base. At another entrance, below, we framed the sign by washing the Ocotillo, Optuntia, Dasylirion, and Yucca that surround it on both sides.

Disruptive Technology Causes New Learning   **Not Just Another Light Source**

Rio Verde Community Entrances

Above, the main entrance at Four Peaks Boulevard is flanked with two scenes on the sides and a median strip with the sign. We uplighted the trees and Saguaros, lit the stone base for the sign brighter than the surrounding street entrances, and downlit the flanking scene walls and desert shrubs in front. This is all using Excelsior Lighting, (excelsiorlighting.com), fixtures originally designed for halogen MR16, MR11, or MR8 lamps, but with LED replacement lamps from 7.5 watts at 60° beam spread down to 2.5 watt, 60° beam spread lamps. It doesn't take much, and, even though LED is more efficient than old technology halogen, using such low wattage, the amount of light we use does not obscure the black night sky.

Not Just Another Light Source *Disruptive Technology Causes New Learning*
SECTION III
Introducing the Michael System by HKUSA Lighting Group

Hiroshi Kira asked me to help him design a prototype installation for the Michael System. He and Michael Hooker had discussed this idea for many years. After Michaels' death, Hiroshi and his engineers designed this system for designers to have their lighting system become animated over seven hours. These 14 images show how the 20 control zones vary.

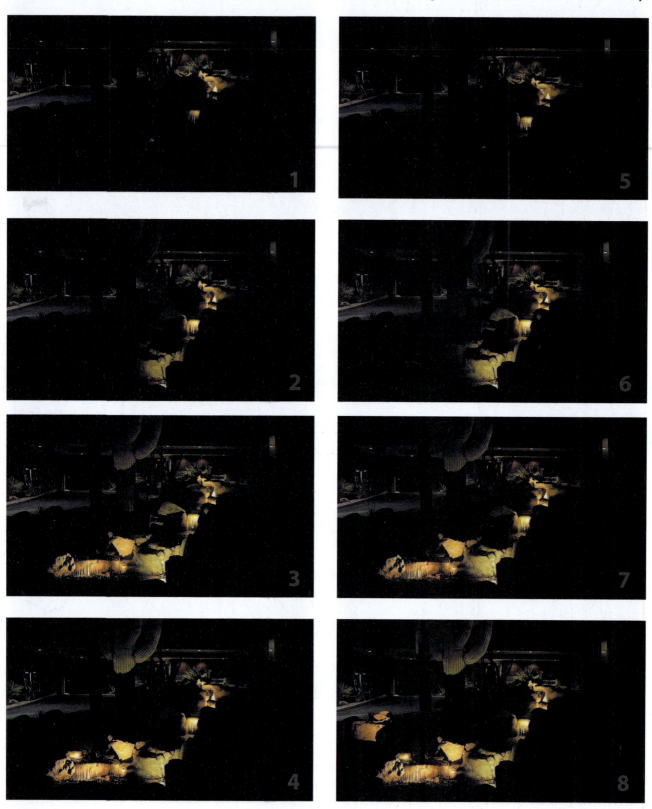

Disruptive Technology Causes New Learning **Not Just Another Light Source**

Introducing the Michael System by HKusa Lighting Group

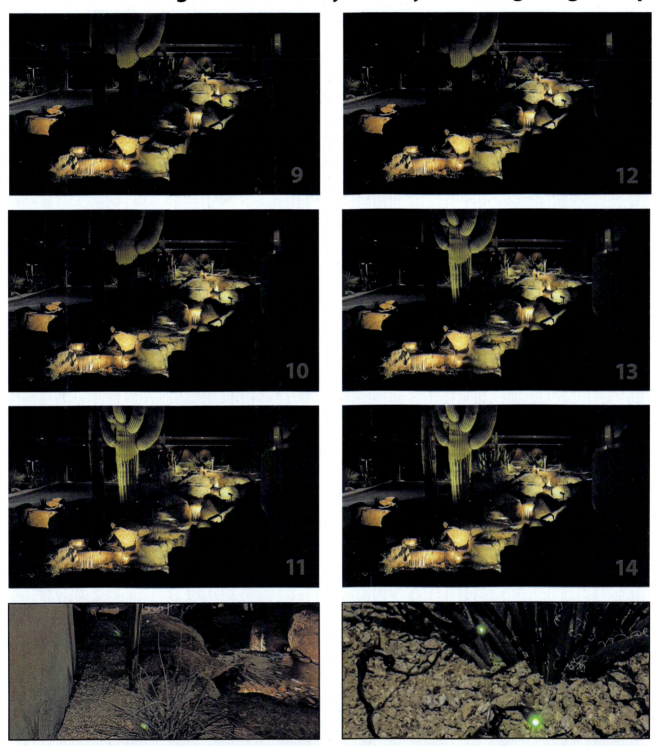

Starting by revealing the waterfall in stages; then adding the rock formation surrounding it, then adding top lighting from the rise, then the Saguaro and it's very top, and finally a cactus in the distance; the system varies the lighting during the time the adjacent club restaurant patio is open for dining. When only the waterfall lights are activated, firefly lights twinkle for a few minutes, reminding all the Midwesterner residents or 'snowbirds' of their childhood. Ed Ehinger and his team, designed the garden.
3E&WWG Companies, Fort Wayne, Indiana, 3e-industries.com. 260-244-0050.
Hiroshi Kira. hklightinggroup.com. 805-480-4881.

Not Just Another Light Source *Disruptive Technology Causes New Learning*
SECTION III

Arizona Thrives On Outdoor Living

Disruptive Technology Causes New Learning   **Not Just Another Light Source**

Arizona Thrives On Outdoor Living

In the Sonoran Desert it gets dark fairly early every night of the year, giving us plenty of time to enjoy the night. Backyard rooms here are designed with gracious entrances, often with pools, hot tubs, and water features. There are simple or elaborate grilling areas, multiple seating and dining locations. The rooms are meant to be lived in as much as night as during the day.

Kirk Bianchi designed this backyard garden. Entering through the heavy metal gate (no javelinas, please), you walk through the desert planting toward the pool and raised hot tub. Kirk often incorporates walls that separate various outdoor living spaces. Here, using a strong color, shown by the back lighting of the Lophocereus marginatus or Fencepost Cactus, draws you in.

Plantings surrounding the activity areas have multiple uplights and downlights to show the land-sculpting, the use of rocks, and the plants. The side lighting of the yellow barrel grouping, lower left, shows the texture of the spines and their flowering area tufts. Above, the agave has a wash of uplight and then a ring mount fixture in the background tree lights down into it's center to show the leaf form, leaf color, and its serrated edging, along with the Ocotillo texture.

bianchidesign.com, kirk@bianchidesign.com, 480-314-0048

Not Just Another Light Source *Disruptive Technology Causes New Learning*
SECTION III

Arizona Thrives On Outdoor Living

The daytime shot shows you Kirks' playing with form and color in his wall planning. Then, below, how we incorporated that feature of the design at night with light on the middle wall from a fixture mounted on and behind the right wall. The dark left wall is getting wash light, from the left, that is generally lighting that area.

Disruptive Technology Causes New Learning **Not Just Another Light Source**
SECTION III

Arizona Thrives On Outdoor Living

This pair of photos show how the colored pool lighting changes the appearance and feeling of the space. Perhaps more lively with the pool lighting, when the pool lighting is off, the spaces feels quieter and you see the plantings reflecting in the water's surface. Note how we grazed the edge of the raised hot tub, showing its wetness and texturing.

Not Just Another Light Source *Disruptive Technology Causes New Learning*
SECTION III
Lighting Expands Your Outdoor Living Space

Arizona gardens balance between natural desert and outdoor living spaces. Many gardens use artificial turf for green space not requiring water. Surprisingly, many trees thrive here, native or Australian, providing downlighting capability. The tall tree, Aloe Hercules, at the end of the pool, benefits from downlighting as does the overall garden, showing more ground plane. Uplighting creates wonderful shadow patterns on walls.

Disruptive Technology Causes New Learning   **Not Just Another Light Source**
SECTION III

Lighting Expands Your Outdoor Living Space

Seeing the reflections in the pool surface always delights. Multiple downlights show ground plane plants in both beds, the top of the Tree aloe, plus the mesquite tree's trunk/branching structure. The front left of the tree juts forward toward the pool, so uplighting that portion wasn't easily accomplished. We decided to leave it dark, allowing your eye to move between the tree, Aloe and the Saguaro. Those three elements, tree, Aloe, and Saguaro comprise the main focal elements, allowing your eye to move easily between them which translates to visual comfort in this outdoor living space.

Not Just Another Light Source *Disruptive Technology Causes New Learning*
SECTION III
Lighting Expands Your Outdoor Living Space

Another Kirk Bianchi landscape design, this day to night pair shows how we made the space easily usable and enjoyable at night. As with many of my clients, these owners enjoy their garden at least as much at night, if not more, than during the day, especially in the winter. Most of this hardscape benefits from either tree- or ring-mount downlights, increasing the sense of space, and how to move safely through the garden.

Disruptive Technology Causes New Learning   **Not Just Another Light Source**
SECTION III

Lighting Expands Your Outdoor Living Space

I try to include simple details in all projects. Here one downlight over the cactus in the blue pot provides task lighting for understanding changes in elevation. Building mounted downlights show the stair case and plantings outside the living room windows. All together, the balance of light levels gives the diners on the upper terrace a beautiful scene to enjoy.

Not Just Another Light Source *Disruptive Technology Causes New Learning*
SECTION III
Lighting Expands Your Outdoor Living Space

Looking from either the informal cocktail seating or the dining areas on the upper patio, this view directly across the pool onto the golf course is stunning. Normally two objects like these existing palms and the Saguaro don't provide visual stability, but, I couldn't leave the Saguaro unlit. A big, native specimen, hundreds of years old, it has three uplights to show three dimensions and all those arms.

Disruptive Technology Causes New Learning   **Not Just Another Light Source**
SECTION III

A Garden for Sculpture

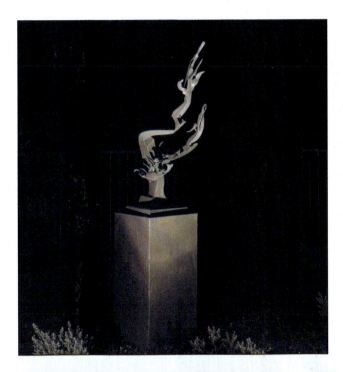

Gardens often have sculpture; this one was designed for this portion of the owners' art collection. Each one lit to show it's form, including the Pachycereus weberi 'Toothpick', cactus at right, as the owner fondly refers to it. After he purchased that specimen and had it planted between two trees, I respectfully asked if I could add lighting for it! Grazing each sculpture, often from multiple positions, the texture of the long cactus spines show clearly.

Another Bianchi Design project, Kirk planned this garden layout to showcase each sculpture with cohesion across the garden. Then, with a space available at the end of the sitting patio, the owner planted the cactus. Over the years, I have found that one of a couple is more interested in lighting. True here too, it was 'him' in this case. When 'the other party' sees the results, they always love their night space. She raves over the night garden she hadn't imagined.

Not Just Another Light Source *Disruptive Technology Causes New Learning*
SECTION III

A Garden for Sculpture

The view out their master bedroom window captivates her. She has the controls set so that she gets to drift off to sleep viewing this and wakes up in the morning before dawn to see it again. Kirk planned a series of curving walls to embrace each sculpture, providing separation, along with cohesion from the rhythm of the walls across the back garden. Downlights at the eaves reveals the seated man sculpture and planting beds, providing information about the edges of hardscape across the space. Throughout, we carefully located uplights, downlights, or aimable fixtures mounted on/behind walls providing horizontal light to show the shape, form, and juxtaposition along the series of walls. I always suggest using more fixtures and less wattage - it makes creating this kind of visual impact in a night garden.

Disruptive Technology Causes New Learning **Not Just Another Light Source**
SECTION III

A Garden for Sculpture

In these Arizona gardens, I often include element(s) outside the property wall, including the tree behind the Saguaros above. Looking at the upper right, that is the view as you enter the garden from the front, looking along three sculptures. Planting beds planned at each of the roof overhang columns provides a downlight location that doubles as task lighting, provides cohesion across the view, and high lighting the wonderful texture of that Cereus peruvianus 'Monstrose'.

Not Just Another Light Source *Disruptive Technology Causes New Learning*
SECTION III
George Calls It the Last Resort

George's and my garden in Rio Verde, AZ provides us with beautiful scenes day and night. The decisions about what to light and what to leave dark is a decision we face on every project. Above, I wanted just a little backdrop around the lion/bowl planter which required downlighting for the plant plus uplighting on both sides to show the draping form of the Russelia equisetiformis/Fire Cracker plant. The bird sculpture moved back from NY to it's home, AZ, and while important, it is no longer the star, sharing that role with the Acacia stenophylla/Shoestring Acacia.

Disruptive Technology Causes New Learning **Not Just Another Light Source**
SECTION III

George Calls It the Last Resort

Arriving at our Casa Saluki, the gates usher you into the front patio. Existing sconces line the walls providing general lighting that complements humans in space. Existing downlights fill in the width of the space. As with most gardens, the grounds here are in constant flux and building the lighting scenes has taken years of repair and replacement of much existing infrastructure and fixtures. Of course with many additions to fill out the scenes in the multiple garden spaces, the maintenance never ends.

Not Just Another Light Source *Disruptive Technology Causes New Learning*
SECTION III

George Calls It the Last Resort

From the street, I sculpted the arrival view, leaving some things dark or very soft. Original pathlights provide walkway lighting. I needed to make sure that your eye goes to the silhouetted Saluki sculptures, inside the gates, leading you to the front door. Creating the balance has taken multiple sessions, deciding light level at each element and whether an element gets light at all. Inside the front patio, I relamped existing fixtures to LED, carefully balancing for a cohesive scene, and then dimming the overall scene using the whole house control system.

Disruptive Technology Causes New Learning   **Not Just Another Light Source**
SECTION III

George Calls It the Last Resort

Multiple lighting zones allow setting various scenes depending on patio use. These existing festoon lights provide general fill and party atmosphere. Without them, the scene is quieter. The overall lighting scene, once the lighting zones are balanced, can be dimmed. Having the ability to raise all parts of the scene, allows raising the landscape lighting for view from inside when we're home alone. The gold neon back lighting of the Saluki wall sculpture (Ben Livingston) creates it's silhouette (less dramatic here than on our New York garage (– see page 311).

Not Just Another Light Source *Disruptive Technology Causes New Learning*
SECTION III
George Calls It the Last Resort

The view from the patio to the left, above, is a non-formal scene with multiple elements lit to show their characteristics, but no focal point. Looking back toward the patio, the Ocotillo has enough light to highlight it's form. Opposite lower, the Ocotillo was lit by Michelle Mueller and me, during a mockup session one year, showing the vivid color of GLL products.

Disruptive Technology Causes New Learning   **Not Just Another Light Source**
SECTION III

George Calls It the Last Resort

Throughout the property I have used downlighting to show the overall garden feeling, with notes of special experiences, such as the multiple stem Yucca showing in the East Garden from the street front garden view.

Not Just Another Light Source *Disruptive Technology Causes New Learning*
SECTION III

George Calls It the Last Resort

Every locale has it's native trees; one in AZ is the Desert Ironwood/Olneya tesota. Typically multiple trunk, these become massive trees and are great for landscape lighting, providing downlighting locations. The central tree in our drive area, this one has more downlights than uplights. I wanted to show the amazing cactus specimens in the drive circle, and the driveway surrounding the tree limited my uplighting scope. The Ironwood, left outside the drive gates, is softer, to not detract from that amazing scene. It has a story of responding to change: one of landscape lighting's constant issues.

Disruptive Technology Causes New Learning **Not Just Another Light Source**
SECTION III

George Calls It the Last Resort

Above left, an uplight covers part of the front canopy and provides uplighting to the leaves undersides. Adding a ring mount downlight, (see the red circle above), over the Agave top, shows it's spikey form. One day, top right, this massive flower stalk started, it grew up through the tree canopy, and, then, as all Agaves do, the plant died (it took about 6 months for the flowering). So, losing that very large plant, what did I do? A maintenance issue we have to deal with constantly.

Many Agaves produce pups from their main root stem as they grow and this one did. In this lower photo, you can see the new pup growing – compare old and new ones; this one has years of growing to reach the other's size. The existing lighting worked, requiring no changes, other than reaiming a bit, with the rock now being more important in the view until the Agave grows over it, as the old one did.

Not Just Another Light Source *Disruptive Technology Causes New Learning*
SECTION III

George Calls It the Last Resort

Another Sonoran Desert native: the Palo Verde/ Cercidium microphyllum tree (as with other genus, there are many species). Another typically multi-trunk tree with a green bark, I have highlighted the trunk here with the canopy softer. Cordia boissieri/ Texas Olive, below, blooms spring-fall. Dense leaves with dense leaf overlap suggests lighting from outside the canopy.

Disruptive Technology Causes New Learning   Not Just Another Light Source
SECTION III

George Calls It the Last Resort

In the lower photo, here in March 2020, we had a five night freeze that killed top leaves; they grew back. Aloe blooms start in winter under it's canopy. Above, I placed three pots with downlighting on the stage bench to balance with the massive Texas Olive. That lighting doubles for accenting performances on the stage during events.

Not Just Another Light Source *Disruptive Technology Causes New Learning*
SECTION III

George Calls It the Last Resort

Throughout the gardens, I set up mini-compositions – here the Yucca, Palo Verde, and the lizard that blend into other mini-compositions for cohesion throughout the gardens from multiple viewing angles. The lizard tongue, lit with an uplight mounted to a rock behind the shrub, while showing the tongue, also creates texture and brightness on the rock.

Disruptive Technology Causes New Learning **Not Just Another Light Source**
SECTION III

Indoor and Outdoor Lighting Can Work Together

Landscape lighting typically is softer than interior lighting. We have to think about all the issues of each project and how the owners use their property. Here, my dear friends, Karen and Dana, love to have guests for dinner. Karen, (karen@libbydesign.com), a designer, planned this glass shelf system, allowing her plantings to show through the house wall. We had to provide enough light across the window's width so that diners got to see the wonderful garden surrounding their dinner. This harkens back to my first landscape lighting project: her mom's living room (see page 1).

To produce landscape lighting as art, we need to think about the global issues of the project. How each area relates to another; how our clients use the property, or may use it once we bestow lighting; how ALL the plants will grow over time, not just the ones we plan to light; of course, always being thoughtful about the initial budget, maintenance, and electrical costs.

Using our art skills honed from testing in the field; borrowing techniques from theatre lighting regarding how we light people and sculpture and how we use darkness and shadow to complete our compositions; keeping our eye on details that may not seem important – that lizard's tongue! Using that uplight, I grazed the rock, before the light hit the tongue, as part of the framing for that focal point, with the framing actually being brighter than the light on the lizard's back. One thing I learned from six years of studying Latin: we need to know when to break the rules.

International Landscape Lighting Institute
Teaching Via the Intensive Course

Explaining the Intensive Course

Starting in the 1980s, I taught at UC Berkeley in Landscape Architecture. I convinced my swim club to let us use their grounds for lighting mockups. Later, I simultaneously taught at Rutgers, and Naomi Miller, then teaching at RPI, asked if I would design a hands-on course. That became the Intensive Course for the educational nonprofit, the International Landscape Lighting Institute, that I founded in 2010. All attendees and mentors receive big course binders.

Project of: **International Landscape Lighting Institute**			**Lead Mentors**: 1.Emily Gorecki, 2.Chris Mitchell, 3. Jim Ply		
Guest Instructors: Mark Schulkamp, Donald Bradley, Dr. David Brearey, George Gruel, Jack Magai			**Shadows & Dedicated Rovers**: 1.Ken Simons & Ramona Dimon; 2. Katie Wilsey & Scott Williams; 3. Brooke Silber & Brooke Perin; **Boomerangs**: Jesse Loucks, Ken Martin, Rick Dekeyser, Ron Carter		
1st Day — Friday September 19, 2014	Location: Saluki Park, Brunswick, NY		Dates	Friday September 19 through Tuesday September 23, 2014	Dark by: 7:20-7:30PM
Instructors	Class Location	Lecture, Workshop, & Site Sessions	Time:	8:00AM — 5:30PM	8.0 Daytime Class hours
All instructors, Mentors, Shadows, Rovers, & Boomerangs	Class room	Introductions and review the course		8:00AM — 8:30AM	30 minutes
Jan, All	Class room	Lecture: Lamps — the tool that allows us to create effects (Chapters 2 & 6)		8:30AM — 9:30AM	1.0 hours	15 minute break
Jan & Don, All	Class room	Demonstration: Comparison and variation of lamps for landscape use		9:45AM — 11:15AM	1.5 hours
Jan, All	Class room	Lecture: Site Review & Client Interview (Chapter 1)		11:15AM — 11:45AM	30 minutes
Jan & George, All	Site	Project Site Walk through & Teams Pick Mockup Site: Advise Jan asap for selection (equipment delivered to your area after selection- unless raining, then setup under tents in driveway for tonights lamp testing session)		11:45AM — 12:15AM	30 minutes
Jan & Don, All	Studio Garage	Review our equipment Setup		12:15PM — 12:30PM	15 minutes
Lunch	Studio Kitchen & Deck		Time:	12:30PM — 1:30PM	1.0 hour
Jan & Don	Class room	Lecture & Demonstration: Fixtures, the holder of the lamp — discuss construction & important considerations in selection (Chapters 7 & 8)		1:30PM — 2:45PM	1.25 hours
Jan	Class room	Organize mockup and aiming session discussion — review night session assignment — **Let Jan know if you will want fixtures mounted in trees for your mockup presentation** —		2:45PM — 3:15PM	30 minutes	Jan Call Jack by end of day
Teams with Jan & George	Site	Groups : 'Client' Interview in your area; Start preparing equipment 'Kit' for night assignment & plan team tasks; Start initial sketches of your area		3:15PM — 5:30PM	2.25 hours	15 minute break
Relax/Refresh/Dinner	Studio Kitchen & Deck		Time:	5:30PM — 6:30PM	1.0 hours
1st Night	Site		Time:	6:30PM — 10:30PM	4.0 Night Class hours
Teams	Site	Attendees **experiment with lamps**: DON'T start laying-out or mocking-up your area's lighting design		6:30PM — 8:30PM	2.00 hours
Teams	Site	Each group demo/present 1 thing learned tothe rest of class: 15 minutes each		8:30PM - 9:15PM	45 minutes
Teams	Site	Clean up area for the night		9:15PM — 9:30PM	15 minutes
Jan & Don, All	Site	Demonstration at and of the Landscape Lighting Exhibition - SHOW THE USE OF EACH UPLIGHT FOR THE BLACK WALNUT PAIR - halogen and LED		9:30PM — 10:30PM	1.0 Hour

Attendance was limited to 15 allowing everyone to play with the multitude of lamps and fixtures. We all met the evening before the course started so that everyone was ready for the roughly 12-hour course for each of five days and four nights. These two pages from the outline give you a sense of the rigor of the course. Note above that on the first day we need to alert our arborist how many fixtures he will need to temporarily install in trees for the public lighting reveal on the final evening.

Teaching Via the Intensive Course **International Landscape Lighting Institute**

SECTION IV

Explaining the Intensive Course

4th Day — Monday September 22, 2014				
Instructors	Class Location	Lecture / Workshop / Site Sessions	Time: 8:30AM — 5:30PM	7.50 Daytime Class hours
Jan	Class room	Techniques Lecture: Lighting Paths & Stairs, Sculptures, Water features, & Architectural Structures (Chapters 16, 17, 18, & 19)	8:30AM — 10:30AM	2.00 hours
Teams	Site	Finalize Design Ideas, Setup and Documentation including: Layout, Lamping, Transformer, Loads, and Control Strategy — Review with your mentor; Mark/Don, Jesse/Tony, then Jan	10:30AM — 12:30PM	2.00 hours / 15 minute break
Lunch	Studio Kitchen & Deck	"Class" Photo by pond (please wear your vest!)	Time: 12:30PM — 1:30PM	1.00 hours
Teams	Site	Finalize design setup and aiming; work on presentation approach for last night — Review with mentor team	1:30PM — 4:15PM	2.75 hours
		Mentor Teams: Get your teams documents to GEORGE by 4:00PM for him to scan to show everyone during the review session tomorrow morning.		15 minute break
		Any equipment pulled from the equipment inventory in the garage that is not being used - return before dinner; any equipment from the team cases get cleaned up and return to the cases by the end of the night.		
Jan	Class room	Contract & Record Documentation – What the contractor needs to build your design and what the client needs to keep the system functioning as intended (Ch 4 & 5)	4:15PM — 5:30PM	1.25 hours
Relax/Refresh/Dinner	Studio Kitchen & Deck		Time: 5:30PM — 7:00PM	1.50 hours
4th Night	Site		Time: 7:00PM — 10:30PM	3.50 Night Class hours
Teams	Site	Finalize Adjustments	7:00PM — 8:00PM	1.00 hours
Teams, All	Site	**Group MockUp Presentations - 20 minutes each**	8:00PM — 9:00PM	1.00 hours
Teams	Site	Photography session with George Gruel and clean up area for the night	8:00PM — 10:30PM	2.50 hours
ALL	Tent on the lawn	Reception with the public - tea, coffee, cookies, cupcakes and discussion - keep the mockups on until the end.	9:00PM — 10:30PM	1.5 hours

Just before lunch on the first day, we review the equipment each team receives – six road cases of fixtures, transformers and cables with quick-release connections, plus multiple cases of lamps. The amount of equipment covers the breadth of both fixtures and lamps available each year (taking us months to update every spring prior to that year's course).

International Landscape Lighting Institute *Teaching Via the Intensive Course*
SECTION IV
Explaining the Intensive Course

Our first year, 2006 (before becoming a nonprofit), we had four attendees and I taught the entire class. As class sizes quickly grew, I asked previous attendees to become instructors and mentors. By 2012, we realized we needed a team of mentors for anyone to complete the course. When forming design teams, I tried to include someone that understood electricity, someone that knew about plants, and someone with some experience in lighting. Teams of five would work together. Their Lead Mentor coordinated with other groups to ensure the teams created visual cohesion across the site. Once the teams picked their area, even in the rain, mentors delivered all their equipment to their site using this trailer to deliver it as quickly as possible. Attendee teams then start laying out their equipment to make it ready once it's dark.

The first night, they test their fixtures and lamps to get a sense of what they can do. The following day, they start imagining their design and get it ready for the second night of testing. Each night they present their ideas for feedback from instructors and mentors and to share with the other teams. By the third night, everyone is scrambling to fix their earlier attempts and get it all ready for their public presentations on the last night. We eventually got an AV system and had Pam Morris and Karen Libby training us all on how to present walking backwards in the dark to keep eye contact with our audience of typically over 100.

Teaching Via the Intensive Course **International Landscape Lighting Institute**
SECTION IV

Explaining the Intensive Course

From the early classes at RPI, I learned that no one wanted to stop working on their design mockup and they would keep working late into the night. Keeping them well fed was imperative. The course outline had little time for relaxing, even during meals, so our sponsoring manufacturers used that time to familiarize attendees and mentors with the their line and new equipment. Our chef, Debbie Freinberg, and Jan Moyer Design support staff made sure that meals went smoothly and that all guests had whatever they needed during this frantic time.

The Salukis were always a part of the experience, participating in all aspects of the course. That limited relaxation time, during breaks and meals, led to strong bonds being forged between attendees and mentors. They remain close and help each other on projects to this day. ILLI continues today, though side-lined during COVID-19 along with everything in our lives across our planet. The mentors continue to carry on the spirit of the course since I had to step down from running it in 2016. ILLI continues to share information to raise the bar, providing sensitive lighting for all.

International Landscape Lighting Institute *Teaching Via the Intensive Course*
SECTION IV
Explaining the Intensive Course

Everyone pitches in during the mockup sessions to get the designs as complete and perfect as possible. Especially with inexperienced attendees, initial attempts have too much light and/or not enough fixtures to actually create what they imagine in their minds. They need to create record documents of their design with power distribution, transformer loading, each fixture's location and its lamping, which help them to learn the importance of this information for maintenance and future expansion on their projects – it inevitably happens and that information saves them time and effort down the road.

After Mark Schulkamp designed/ donated a trailer for faster equipment delivery (see page 238), we added tents to shield everything from the weather, foldable tables providing work area, and task lighting for the equipment cases.

Teaching Via the Intensive Course **International Landscape Lighting Institute**

Explaining the Intensive Course

The instruction consisted of lectures building upon themselves, demonstrations of lamps, wiring, working with arborists, and Dr. David Brearey teaching and pruning in the teams' areas. A large part of landscape lighting is being prepared in the field –setting up equipment and ladders, making sure arborists, lines are stable in the trees, and pre-setting/aiming fixtures in trees before dark. We needed then, and still today, to share this critical knowledge with lighting designers, installers, and with the arborists.

International Landscape Lighting Institute *Teaching Via the Intensive Course*
SECTION IV
Explaining the Intensive Course

Above you see Don Bradley and me presenting multiple lamping options to help attendees become familiar with the color, beams pread, quality, and quantity of light various lamps produce. Variation in color, light output, and beam spread between manufacturers needs to be understood before lighting designers purchase drop-in lamps or integral modules. We would show many types of lamps that are used for varying purposes so the design teams could choose between everything in their cases. Their mentors help them design but don't tell them what to do. The teams need to learn what works best for them and this opportunity gives them in-depth knowledge to take back to their projects.

Sponsoring manufacturers, here John Tremaine of Q-Tran (also a former ILLI Board President), bring their equipment to demonstrate, so that the teams understand its benefits and how to use it, as their equipment would be in those multiple cases. Giving the sponsors' access to attendees and mentors produced bonds across the industry. Having good industry connections between designers, installers, manufacturers, and arborists helps everyone, including our clients.

Teaching Via the Intensive Course **International Landscape Lighting Institute**

Explaining the Intensive Course

Each night the teams test their ideas, starting with installing their power distribution and then testing their fixtures and the lamps they wanted to see. Their sites are large, giving them the opportunity to learn how to light large mature trees and groups of trees creating a backdrop, as in the pond above; the importance of visually tying the canopy of trees to the ground by lighting the trunks, showing texture of bark. There are so many details that make up successful lighting and almost no one understands the complexity when they start.

Each night the teams show each other their progress and discuss the challenges that they are working out. Having this hands-on access to equipment with instructors and mentors guiding their design development provides them with an immense amount of understanding to work with on their own projects. Having access to arborists to learn about mounting fixtures in trees expands their capabilities in creating a solid visual composition. All designers have differing design sense and working with a team of designers expands their ideas and helps them understand how much of a team effort landscape lighting is in the real world. Teams consist of owners, landscape and/or interior designers, often other lighting designers doing the interior of the project, lighting representatives, distributors, contractors, and manufacturers. All these players efforts need to be integrated into each project.

International Landscape Lighting Institute *Teaching Via the Intensive Course*
SECTION IV
Explaining the Intensive Course

After three nights of mockup and four days of instructions and demonstrations, the teams present their design to the public, no matter where the class is located. Utilizing red flashlights to not impact their designs, each member of the team presents a portion of their design, including their conceptual ideas, the types of fixtures and lamps they used, the total wattage load, how they envision the controls, and describing all the aspects of their design.

Their designs are mockups, so they need to explain to the guests how an actual installation will vary in equipment from what is used in the mockups. For example, they need to explain that fixtures located in grass would become below-grade fixtures with limited aiming flexibility which defines fixture locations.

Having all team members participate in the presentation gives them experience in presenting their ideas to clients during real projects. Many are reluctant, some defer and don't participate. Those that do start to build confidence.

Teaching Via the Intensive Course International Landscape Lighting Institute
SECTION IV

Explaining the Intensive Course

Invited teams participated in designing and building the first ILLI permanent installation. This allowed classes to see lighting surrounding a home and present landscape lighting to visiting public groups. For the presentation nights, a tent was set up for the final dinner, with guests and sponsors invited for refreshments after the presentation.

Above left, multiple sponsors BK Lighting President, Ron Naus, and Regional Sales Manager, Karen Duffy, discuss lighting's future in 2012 during the course.

Lower, right, Craig Klomparens, President of Dauer Manufacturing, meets with mentors and attendees at our Ridgewood, NJ course in 2016. Hearing from the heads of lighting companies about their philosophy and how their equipment is built makes a strong impression.

International Landscape Lighting Institute *Teaching Via the Intensive Course*
SECTION IV

Design Teams Need to Work Together

Each mentoring team guides all aspects of getting through the Intensive Course. They provide their teams the discipline to work through all the requirements of their mockup, including keeping updating the equipment they use for their Record Documents they submit for class review on the last day. George takes photos of their final designs to accompany the documents in those final day discussions. The mentors make sure teams use their time wisely and stop in time for the next demonstration, lecture, each meal. Each day the mentors encourage the team to interact with the other teams and visit their mockup sites to ensure that the overall property looks visually cohesive on the presentation night. This helps designers consider various areas of any client site, small or large, planning their overall lighting to blend from one area to another, whether close by or separated by distance.

These three photos from differing years, 2008 above; two 2012 classes at right (early October, Class 1 photo, lower; and a late October Class 2 photo, upper), exemplify the effort to have all areas of a project work together. Notice the difference in Maple trees in the distance in both at right over the course of a few weeks. Plant materials may change dramatically from season to season. Designers need to include that in their planning for projects.

Seeing how different design teams can create a cohesive scene within their area and then how with varying designers that can translate from one area to another, helps us all learn the importance of ensuring that all areas of a site work together for our clients.

Teaching Via the Intensive Course International Landscape Lighting Institute
SECTION IV

Design Teams Need to Work Together

International Landscape Lighting Institute *Teaching Via the Intensive Course*
SECTION IV

Groups of Trees Create a Night Space

In this 2012 scene, the team decided to downplay the big tree but didn't let it go dark – in the middle, behind the two trees which they lit as focal points. Notice the soft light on the back tree's trunk and the downlighting around that tree providing visual connection to the two front trees, and downlighting in all three provides 'ground plane' lighting showing the full scene.

Here and at the right are two views from 2008 – this page's photos show a more distant view and the photo on the next page, a close-up view along the stream. Above, photo provides a comfortable scene as you approach the back deck of my studio. Then at right, standing near the top of the stream looking down the stream. The designers used a combination of path lights to show the stream, with uplights grazing the grasses so that the length of the stream is enjoyable. The color of trees varies, as shown here, with the Birches warm, while the Picea pungens/Colorado Blue Spruce has an inherent blue color. Using white light on both, in this case halogen, which is warm, the trees' natural colors show. In the lower photo on this page, this team's use of downlights for ground plane shows the color of fall annuals. Using this technique across this scene provides continuity.

Teaching Via the Intensive Course   **International Landscape Lighting Institute**
SECTION IV

Groups of Trees Create a Night Space

International Landscape Lighting Institute *Teaching Via the Intensive Course*
SECTION IV

Groups of Trees Create a Night Space

2009 marked the year that, for the first time, one team chose to light one tree in their scene entirely with LED. This photo includes two areas. The furthest left tall tree is the one lit with LED. Even with two very different light sources, these designs work together in overall effect for the trees and light level across the two scenes. The lighting levels are not, 'the same', on one tree or element, but within the comfort of a 3:1 brightness ratio. Notice how much downlighting both teams are using. Downlighting shows the ground plane helping people understand their surroundings, providing a sense of visual comfort after dark.

This 2014 team wanted the entrance to George's studio to welcome and show the two activity areas on either side of the building: a dining area on the left and art area at right. Their use of lit trees surrounding the building frames the building and its activity areas, including light at the back patio, making the entire grounds usable.

Teaching Via the Intensive Course   **International Landscape Lighting Institute**
SECTION IV

Groups of Trees Create a Night Space

In another area of the six acres at Saluki Park, used from 2006 through 2014 for ILLI courses, this team lights the area adjacent to the Oddstick School building (George's studio most of the year, until ILLI classes take over the entire property for a week). Look closely and you can see George's studio through the Birches on the left. This team melded the pond area and back of my studio with the other teams. They provide light for you to enjoy the birch reflecting in the pond surface and visually connect the front entrance and back deck of the my studio, at right.

Notice that in these and all the team scenes, it is black night in the sky. What gets revealed carves out a night living space without overwhelming the darkness of night. Landscape lighting uses so little wattage or light output to retain and respect the night skies. All three of these scenes provide humans with the enjoyment of these grounds. I loved the majesty of the trees throughout these six acres. Looking at the upper left photo, with views from multiple patios and the sleeping porch at the top of the stairs, which of those trees could be left unlit without disrupting the scene?

Part of lighting design includes the controls strategy. Lighting can comprise multiple zones and they can be activated separately. For example, the arrival lights at the Odd Stick Studio can be one zone, either controlled by time on a whole house system or an astronomic (tracking time change) timer to be left on for so many hours a day. One or more zones or scenes can be controlled independently by timer or local device. Lighting does not have to be on every night or from dusk to dawn. It can be simply turned on when desired.

International Landscape Lighting Institute *Teaching Via the Intensive Course*
SECTION IV

Groups of Trees Create a Night Space

This apple orchard was selected by teams many times. In 2010, the mature Acer saccharum/Sugar Maple has begun to show its fall color, temporarily making it the star. This grouping of Apple and Maple trees shows design flexibility regarding how to approach the orchard. In this mockup, the trees' lighting level is similar, but the color change calls attention to that rear tree. From tree-mounted downlights some of the downlighting is intentional, while some is spill from temporary ground-level mockup fixtures.

Earlier in October 2012, not only had that mature Sugar Maple completely turned and lost leaves, but the Acer rubrum 'October Glory' in front is claiming the spotlight at the moment. The Acer rubrum 'Autumn Radiance', front right, is just starting its color and will draw attention within days. I chose and planted these three maples because they color up, in succession every year, changing the scene composition. Notice how the downlighting under the trees provides rhythm adding to the visual cohesion across this view.

Teaching Via the Intensive Course **International Landscape Lighting Institute**
SECTION IV

Groups of Trees Create a Night Space

Viewed from across the pond, the reflective quality of the water's surface provides differing experiences from multiple views– which happens in any landscape. In a grouping of trees like this, decisions about which trees or elements to light and which to leave dark must be made. This team chose to leave the right tree completely dark and that back left tree they lit only the right side – and softly, providing some background fill. In both this photo and the lower left, the lower plantings along the back border are lit as fill lighting which provides depth and visually connects the bigger trees together in the scene.

Comparing the image above and the lower left on page 252, the trunks of the far left Apple tree and the two Maples at right are brighter, as with most of the lighting. Teams play with brightness relationship and overall lighting during their mockup time. In city scenes, the higher light level, above, may be preferred due to high ambient light levels, while in darker neighborhoods, the lower light levels, lower left, are usually preferred. This team softened the trees for their final presentation.

When you want to see landscape lighting from inside a building, you have to plan how it will appear through interior windows and then think about how that feels when you are in the landscape space. With much higher interior lighting levels for living, you either dim the interior lighting to a very soft level for the lighting to show or provide dimming on the landscape lighting. Dimming allows you to raise the landscape lighting level outside, providing a view through the window, and, then to lower the level to a soft output that feels comfortable while in the gardens at night.

International Landscape Lighting Institute *Teaching Via the Intensive Course*
SECTION IV
Groups of Trees Create a Night Space

Teaching Via the Intensive Course **International Landscape Lighting Institute**
SECTION IV

Groups of Trees Create a Night Space

Three design teams lit this north boundary scene. The gardens continually changed over the years from 2010 to 2014, mostly at human scale: note the three trees that each group chose to use as major elements in the scenes they created.

In the upper left scene, the 2010 team decided to limit the scene by withholding light from the immediate surroundings. However, they chose to light some taller evergreen trees behind the middle tree, the Fagus grandifolia/American Beech, insinuating depth. They used some uplighting and downlighting for the Beech's multi-trunk structure as the brightest level in the scene, bringing the viewer's eye to the ground in the middle of the scene. Then they surrounded the trunks by softly lighting the shrubs around it. As with the other two design teams, they played with the lighting level of the inner branching structure of the left tree, Quercus rubra/Northern Red Oak, and on the right tree, Gleditsia triacanthos/Honey Locust. They lit the multi-trunk stronger than the Oak but softer than the Beech, and the Honey Locust's canopy even more softly but at a slightly higher level on the inside.

Compare that to the lower left, with the 2011 team's approach of highlighting the Beech's trunk/branching structure at the brightest level of all three scenes, with the Oak's front canopy brighter and the Honey Locust's canopy more uneven. The biggest difference is that they do not have the evergreens' lit behind the Beeches but provided more lighting throughout the scene on the ground plane plantings at a brighter level, making this more inviting to go visit, rather than a visual scene in the distance.

Above, in 2014, I noticed that my lighting was getting softer overall, as is this teams' lighting. They had David Brearey prune the Honey Locust's canopy, both raising it up off the ground and opening it up some, so that light goes through it up to the top of the canopy. All three classes were in October, but you can see that all three trees' appearances vary from one year to another. This team's ground plane lighting is cohesive and they lit the two pyramidal shrubs, denoting a new pathway access to a new remote parking area, to the brightest level as a visual cue. They lit the Beech's canopy more on the outside than the other two, with the effect of it looking less heavy, showing more of its form, and creating focal point tension with the path shrubs.

All three are strong compositions with different personality, and an interesting comparison that clearly shows how many differing design ideas can work on the same scene.

International Landscape Lighting Institute *Teaching Via the Intensive Course*
SECTION IV
Saluki Park Mockup Areas – Lighting the Pond

There are a number of specific areas that were open to ILLI design teams each year. Each was used as a test area by many groups over the years, and I want to share the varying approaches for each over the next few pages. A continuing favorite was always the pond. It is a good place to start as it showcases how gardens change over the years through plant growth/ death and owners changing their spaces and activities over time. Above, left, is a 1997 photo of the pond. There are two Ulmus americana/Elm trees between three Betula utilis var. jacquemontii/Himalayan Birch (exceptional white bark) and the Picea pungens/Colorado Blue Spruce (all planted in the 1920s'). They were in decline due to Dutch Elm Disease spreading across the United States.

In an attempt to be proactive, (2001 upper right), a grove of Betula nigra 'Heritage'/Heritage River Birch I had planted in 1998 to replace the two Elms was starting to coalesce. They love being alongside water, so they anchor the north end of the pond. My intent was that by the time both Elms had to be removed, the grove would fill in the hole that would have been left.

During a September 2013 course, above left, you can see the Birch grove has filled in, and I have planted two trees at the south end of the pond. At the left of the team is a, Alnus glutinosa 'Imperialis'/Cutleaf Alder with deeply dissected leaves and elegant, feathery pyramidal shape. Growing to 30'/9 meters plus, it loves being near water. Further south of the pond is a Magnolia acuminata 'Koban Dori'/Koban Dori Cucumber Magnolia with big yellow flowers in the spring.

In the above right photo, at the pond's east side, looking south, you can see that not only was I still planting in 2013, but I had just added a new sitting patio to enjoy the pond. The point of all this description is that landscapes continually evolve. Lighting designers must stay attuned to the development and have power infrastructure allowing for additional fixtures and load without having to dig up the gardens. The big shrub beyond the new patio is a Salix purpurea 'Nana'/Purple Willow that got planted in the late 1990s. Plant guides suggest that it gets to be 5' x 5' (1.5 X 1.5m) at maturity. Here, 8'/2.4m high by nearly 20'/6m wide and still expanding – it also likes being by water and gets runoff from the hillside in all seasons.

Teaching Via the Intensive Course International Landscape Lighting Institute

Saluki Park Mockup Areas – Lighting the Pond

By 2007 the Heritage Birch grove had filled in nicely, and behind it you see that one of the Elms still remains, but it was struggling and was removed not too long after. Ponds continually change. At the edges are rushes that we had to continually pull out, and every year I had to cut the flower stalks in an attempt to limit expansion. The ponds surface had both regular and tropical water lilies, both nearly impossible to control. I and others would spend summers removing waterlily plants to open up the water's surface for fall classes – so that lighting could reflect in it. Some years had more, others less. This pond also had Utricularia vulgens/Common Bladderwort – a suspended free-floating aquatic species with very pretty yellow flowers in summer.

The stream that you see by the Heritage Birch grove was planned and installed in stages, at first as a dry stream bed. Then in 2008, with Don Bradley's and Anthony Archer Wills' assistance, we installed a pump in the pond with the water source set up the hill by the east side of my studio letting the water circulate back to the pond. Notice that the siting patio is not there yet.

Each year, attendees found varying conditions at and around the pond. I kept planting and tried to keep up with cleaning out the pond, even hiring a scuba diver for several years to pull roots from the muddy bottom. Each year design teams got updated plans, so they knew the plants and conditions at the site. In the next few pages, you will see multiple years of designs with many varying conditions, including at least one year with plenty of lily pads still on the pond's surface during the course. Normally by October, when many courses were held, the lilly pads would have disappeared, even if they hadn't been pulled out.

Above you can see the tarps a team has laid out, getting their equipment ready for that night's mockup, even on the near side of the pond. Power distribution for this area came from the back side of my studio just up the hill slightly from the pond. Teams would have multiple extension cords running everywhere. We always had enough power, cords, fixtures, and lamps for any ideas the teams wanted to pursue. The mentor teams assisted in preparing power distribution for teams during lectures so that the teams had enough time to concentrate on their design thinking and setups.

International Landscape Lighting Institute *Teaching Via the Intensive Course*
SECTION IV

Saluki Park Mockup Areas – Lighting the Pond

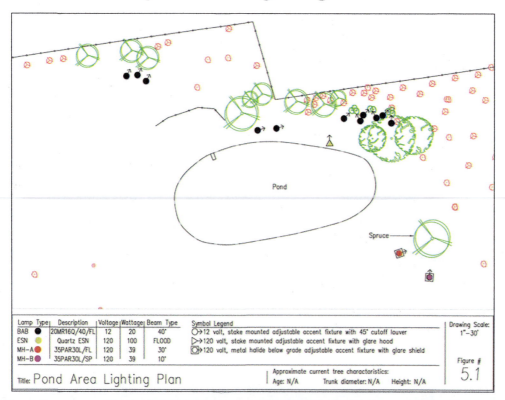

The first pond mockup was done by a team of Lighting Research Center (LRC) students in 1999. Their relatively simple plan was derived from the information given to them that, at that time, there was not much activity, down by the pond. No studios existed yet and the pond was a remote, feature. Their lighting was limited to plants on the west side of the pond and the Spruce – with metal halide lamps to accentuate the tree's blue foliage. Notice the separation between the two lit areas; they intended for the Spruce to be a surprise as you walked down to the pond. They floated candles in the pond giving a sense of its boundaries.

Saluki Park Mockup Areas – Lighting the Pond

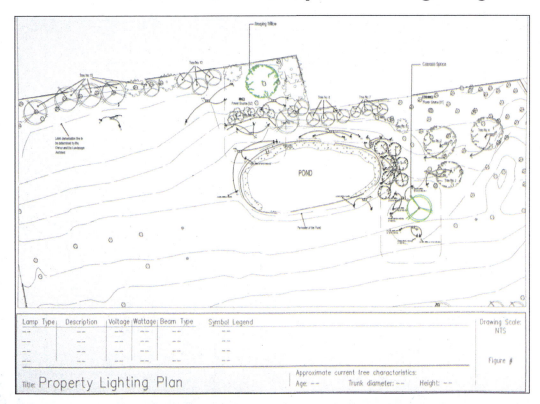

In 2002, LRC students designed an expanded plan, with the rushes highlighted at both the north and south ends of the pond. Their more complete treatment utilized more equipment. They chose to not to intensify the Spruce foliage color, partly because more activity was occurring in that part of the property and they viewed the pond as a more integrated visual scene.

International Landscape Lighting Institute *Teaching Via the Intensive Course*
SECTION IV
Saluki Park Mockup Areas – Lighting the Pond

This view above, still in 2002, from the south end of the pond, shows using the rushes to define the pond's edges. At the north end, this design team lit an Oak furthest north, beyond the two elms. This grouping of three trees filled in the space between the Jacquemontii Birches, lit at left and the Spruce on the right. To coalesce the scene, they grazed the front surface of the Evergreens behind the Birches to the west.

At this early time mockups were held through the LRC at Rensselaer Polytechnic Institute in Troy, NY. After leaving my teaching position there, John Tremaine encouraged me to hold these lighting classes on my own, which started in 2006 until 2010 when ILLI was recognized by the State of New York as a 501(c)3 educational nonprofit.

These students had never lit any landscape spaces before doing these landscape lighting mockups.

The next pond mockup wasn't until 2007, upper right, next page, when this design team expanded even more than the 2003 team incorporating three newly planted Juniperus scopulorum 'Whicita Blue'/Rocky Mountain Junipers. With variation in light level along the western edge of the pond's plantings, these Junipers show strongly due to the contrast of their blue foligage with the rest of the species. This team grazed the rushes from the east side of the pond, filling in the plants on the west side adding to the grazing lights they used to show the conifer's texture. This technique accentuates the lilly pads not removed from the pond's surface that year, but limits walking around the west path.

The team in 2012, next page, lower right, lit the extent of the western edge with a much softer touch. We were all learning that just a little light makes a big statement. It shows the natural appearance, characteristics, even color of plants more comfortably then stronger light. There are always multiple issues at work – softer light works when we are out in the garden, but won't be seen through windows of interior spaces – requiring design and controls decisions.

Teaching Via the Intensive Course   **International Landscape Lighting Institute**
SECTION IV

Saluki Park Mockup Areas – Lighting the Pond

Notice how much prettier the reflections are with no lily pads marring the water's surface, here later in October. Also notice that the Wichita Junipers have grown quite a bit in five years. As with many Evergreens, they have very long limbs, so even simply washing the grouping with one fixture you still see the texture of the foliage. There are multiple new plantings added since the 2007 mockup, and the River Birch grove is starting to have its lower limbs pruned up.

International Landscape Lighting Institute *Teaching Via the Intensive Course*
SECTION IV

Saluki Park Mockup Areas – Lighting the Pond

Looking at three mockups from across the pond, 2008 top, 2010 middle, and 2011 lower, (and both photos on next page), all three teams lit the entire western planting edge and the ostrich sculptures in front of the willow shrub. Each team created complete scenes to enjoy either close-up, at the sitting patio, or from up the hill at the house patios. Yet each design is individual due to varying plantings over those years and the design teams, design sense, their intentions, and their lighting techniques/effects.

Teaching Via the Intensive Course **International Landscape Lighting Institute**
SECTION IV

Saluki Park Mockup Areas – Lighting the Pond

You might notice that the 2011 team used a little color to intensify the Wichita Junipers' color and to shift the foliage color of the Salix babylonica/Weeping Willow behind some tall conifers that they chose not to light. Notice how the Rhus typhina/Velvet Sumac, which colors up early, hasn't in the same time frame in 2011. This team played with three lit glass orbs provided by NightOrbs (info@nightorbs.com, (484-620-2976). Over the days/nights spent developing this scene, they moved the orbs several times, including into the pond. Their vision shifted the plantings' color toward the cooler end of the spectrum, contrasting with the reddish/pink/purple orbs. They grazed the rushes on the east edge with a fixture located to the right aimed along the pond's edge to the south, and washed the west edge of the pond with fixtures located on the eastern shore.

International Landscape Lighting Institute *Teaching Via the Intensive Course*
SECTION IV
Saluki Park Mockup Areas – Lighting the Pond

The 2013 team also used orbs and used warmer color temperature lamps on the plantings, but used intense blue light sources for the heron sculpture, turning it from the rusty-metal sculpture into the blue coloring you see above.
You can see how much pruning has occurred along the back tree line, and it is still evolving. The pruning of lower limbs on the Birches shows the trunks, and these have been individually addressed with grazing light to show the incredible peeling bark that develops as these trees mature.

Teaching Via the Intensive Course   **International Landscape Lighting Institute**
SECTION IV

Saluki Park Mockup Areas – Lighting the Birch Grove

Shifting emphasis now to the Birch grove, look at the difference in the trees from 2001, upper photo, to 2007, lower photo. These trees grow quickly and have more than doubled in both height and width. In 2007, the lower branches have not been cut yet, making their appearance more monolithic as one combined element. Once the lower limbs are removed to show the trunks more, the grove takes on the appearance of multiple individual trees forming a group.

International Landscape Lighting Institute *Teaching Via the Intensive Course*
SECTION IV

Saluki Park Mockup Areas – Lighting the Birch Grove

The 2007 team wanted the lower limbs removed, called '.limbing up'. This pruning has been done above, showing the trunks, revealing that wonderful texture, and changing the appearance from, one, element to a grove consisting of multiple trees. Whether you look straight on from one side or the other, or from the side view, at left along the stream, the trees now show each tree's individuality.

Having this ability to concentrate as deeply as a design team wants on any to every aspect of their area, gives designers the opportunity to get as detailed as they want in their lighting, irrespective of cost; something they may not have the luxury of in their client projects. Spending this effort hones their skills, making them stronger designers whatever their client's budget.

From these two more distant views, or looking more closely at these Birch trees on the next page, these teams think about the trees as artistic elements in an overall art scene. The two images on the next page are by the 2008 team. They graze the trunks, locating fixtures close to the trees to reveal and highlight that amazing peeling bark. There are many kinds of bark – some with interesting color, textured furrows, some with fruits growing on the trunk, others having spines. It pays to study the individual trees comprising a project, so that you understand how the tree will show today and how it may change, as it matures and/or from one season to another.

The upper right photo on the next page shows the Heron sculpture lit with white light, so it's actual rusty metal shows. Notice in all the photos of the Heron, whether here or later in the Apple orchard photos, the designers are thoughtful to light all the characteristics of the bird from its beak to it's tail feathers and its legs.

In the lower right photo on the next page, notice the view to the distant tree...

Teaching Via the Intensive Course   International Landscape Lighting Institute
SECTION IV

Saluki Park Mockup Areas – Lighting the Birch Grove

International Landscape Lighting Institute *Teaching Via the Intensive Course*
SECTION IV
Saluki Park Mockup Areas – Lighting the Birch Grove

Teaching Via the Intensive Course International Landscape Lighting Institute
SECTION IV

Saluki Park Mockup Areas – Lighting the Birch Grove

This sculpture of a heron normally stood here by the north end of the pond and multiple groups chose to light it as a feature in the Birch grove. With permission, some years it would be moved to other areas of the property – typically the Apple orchard. These three heron photos are of three different years, design teams' efforts, upper left 2010, lower left 2011, and above 2013. Each team lights the bird from its head to its feet, showing details the artist gave the bird from its spiral eyes to its metal featherwork and curving, highly-textured neck. This takes multiple fixtures, as many sculptures and most trees require to fully show their characteristics and fine detail. Lighting creates environmental art in your night garden, so giving individual elements this respect creates stronger art, stronger beauty.

Whether the bird is colored or showing its material's color, these designers took the time to consider what the artist's intention – that curving neck is how herons hold their necks. You can have these details show in a scene by choosing fixture location, aiming, brightness, and color, when desired and appropriate. I am not a fan of using colored light, as I prefer to have an element's natural colors show. Above, however, using color to represent the bird's actual color is effective.

Lighting a tree's trunk visually connects the canopy to the ground, so no matter what technique one selects, downlighting to show ground plane or uplighting to be part of the canopy lighting, the bark's characteristics can be revealed. Typically, one uplight on the trunk is necessary, but rarely can it light the overall canopy width by itself. Trees require multiple fixtures for that purpose. They can be outside the canopy as we see above or from underneath the canopy, which is what the team predominantly did in the upper left photo on the previous page. The tree's leaf characteristics guide fixture placement. Birches have dense leaves and dense leaf overlap, but the leaves are somewhat diaphanous – delicate and translucent. Not all leaves are; many are dense and don't transmit light. When this kind of tree has dense leaf overlap, or if the leaves have a brownish color on the underside, you want to locate fixtures outside the canopy to produce light on the canopy's exterior. This isn't always necessary – sometimes you want to light the shape of the canopy from underneath. The tree tells you how to light it, when you take time to observe its characteristics.

International Landscape Lighting Institute *Teaching Via the Intensive Course*
SECTION IV

Saluki Park Mockup Areas – Lighting the Forests

In fall 1999 the exhaustive lawn at Saluki Park extended to the edge of the central forest. I had started planting in front of the forest, determining the shape of a large new planting bed area. An LRC student team chose to light the front edges of the forest trees with metal halide lamps to accentuate the cool color of the Conifers and Rhododenrons from the 1920s. Then they lit the Birches and Oaks with incandescent, intending to draw people into the central opening, leaving the left and right dark.

Teaching Via the Intensive Course **International Landscape Lighting Institute**

Saluki Park Mockup Areas – Lighting the Forests

When they saw it, although it does draw you in, they didn't want that darkness to split the forest in half. So, one Sunday in winter 2000, a big snow storm just dumped snow. I convinced part of the class to come over, including Kevin Simonson, who agreed to photograph in the snow. The team shifted the angle of one HID and felt much happier with the lighting. Look at the snow weighing down those branches, especially on that corner Pinus strobus/White Pine – which lost many branches to snow over the years.

International Landscape Lighting Institute *Teaching Via the Intensive Course*
SECTION IV

Saluki Park Mockup Areas – Lighting the Forests

The 2006 teams took a very different approach, using halogen lamps for everything. The planting bed has been determined with trees and shrubs growing up. The left front tree, in both photos above, was pruned to show trunk and branching structure. The teams continued with the idea of inserting light into the forest opening midway across the forest front. The far right Beech and Oak, above at the north forest end, are the same ones that we saw earlier. Both look great – look at the trunk lighting on the Oak.

Saluki Park Mockup Areas – Lighting the Forests

Again in 2009, the designers inserted light into an opening; this time the entrance into the forest at the far right end between the east and north faces. The Beech and Oak are much softer now and their foliage color better represented due to the underlying blue base of all architectural LED. The Ulmus glabra 'Camperdownii'/Camperdown Elm uplighting shows its umbrella cascading form in front of the Oak.

International Landscape Lighting Institute *Teaching Via the Intensive Course*
SECTION IV
Saluki Park Mockup Areas – Lighting the Forests

By 2011 my studio, reached through that central forest opening, above, had been built and more planting got lit leading to the back door. In 2012, lower photo, the Acer ginnala/Amur Maple has started having a presence as the entry plant with its vibrant green leaves becoming flaming orange in the fall. Pruned up to show its trunk/branching structure, along with a few other specimens left and right, they frame the opening now. All the teams used light inside the forest as a visual destination, including the 2013 team (both upper/lower photos on right page), lighting

Teaching Via the Intensive Course   **International Landscape Lighting Institute**

Saluki Park Mockup Areas – Lighting the Forests

the forest entry at the south end of the forest. They used a bluer-LED on the conifers, except for the uplighting on the visual destination star, Chamaecyparis nootkaensis 'Green Arrow'/Green Arrow Nootkatensis Cypress, framed in the upper photo by the downligting on the two plant holders with orange marigolds in the fall. This team washed the Itea virginica 'Henry's Garnet' sweetspire, starting its red fall color in the front bed. In the lower photo, notice the soft branching pattern this team placed on the forest floor by downlighting branches above.

International Landscape Lighting Institute *Teaching Via the Intensive Course*
SECTION IV

Saluki Park Mockup Areas – Lighting the Forests

Teaching Via the Intensive Course **International Landscape Lighting Institute**

SECTION IV

Saluki Park Mockup Areas – Lighting the Forests

Lighting this south forest entrance occurred many times. In 2008, at top left, although the Nootka Cypress was small, the team realized its visual value while in this juvenile form, and knew it would grow up to be the focal point. Using downlighting, the team introduced the flower pots, the recently planted still young Thuja occidentalis 'Little Giant'/ Little Giant Dwarf Arborvitae evergreen balls, and the entry path together. The way this team lit trees deeper into the forest provides a visual rhythm welcoming investigation.

The 2011 team, the photo on bottom left, included the existing demonstration path lights, making the overall scene more mysterious, without any element being a focal point or visual destination. By lighting the background more fully than either of the other years, that entire area of plantings, as the path turns to the left, serves as the scene's visual destination, until someone makes the turn to the next area along the way,

The Nootka Cypress has grown up a lot by 2013, above, clearly showing its very narrow spiral form now with almost "Dr. Suess" projecting arms. This team has chosen to keep the forest relatively quiet with that "breakup" foliage pattern on the ground filling in between the pots and the focal point Cypress. These designers uplit the front of the planters and used tree downlighting for the flowering marigolds in the planters. Their downlighting touches enough of the Arborvitae balls, showing their shape with their fluffy texture.

International Landscape Lighting Institute *Teaching Via the Intensive Course*
SECTION IV

Saluki Park Mockup Areas – Lighting the Forests

Throughout the six acres of landscaping at Saluki Park, many edges had a forest planted in the 1920s, which I cleaned up and augmented by adding many forest edges. The right side of this forest corner existed and the left side with two kinds of Larix-arcinia/Tamarack and Eurolepsis 'Marschlinii'/Dunkeld Larch got planted in the early 2000s. This 2008 team marked the quiet entranceway by uplighting two conifer trunks; they pruned-up the Amelanchier canadensis/ Serviceberry, at right, including it in the overall uplighting, alternating between washing/grazing the fronts of the Larches and the Conifers.

Teaching Via the Intensive Course **International Landscape Lighting Institute**
SECTION IV

Saluki Park Mockup Areas – Lighting the Forests

The 2012 team, above, lit the trees more individually, creating more variation in the boundary, lighting the Acer rubrum 'Brandywine'/Brandywine Red Maple as if a recent storm hadn't devastated its canopy (temporarily), still slightly brighter than the surrounds. The Juglans nigra/Black Walnut tree furthest right is uplit softly from the front, showing its form and branching structure. The 2013 team, below, later in October, uplit the neighbors' Walnut (with permission) to highlight its form and for downlighting the top of the Thuja plicata/Western Cedar, that are still new and growing.

International Landscape Lighting Institute *Teaching Via the Intensive Course*
SECTION IV

Saluki Park Mockup Areas – Lighting the Black Walnuts

In 2000 LRC students selected areas of Saluki Park to design and mockup landscape lighting for the first time. One group picked these three Juglans nigra/Black Walnuts. As you see in the daytime shot, above, of the single Black Walnut, it has a textured trunk with primarily vertical branches that curve at their ends. Lower left is their first attempt, and, like most novice designs, it is too bright on the trunk – they selected a very narrow spot, which, especially on the single tree, doesn't come close to covering the width of its canopy. On their second attempt, you can see that the trunks on the pair are much better; you can even notice that the trunk is textured, but the light distribution still does not cover the canopy's width. A common misconception about lighting a tall tree is that you need a narrow spot distribution with strong output. This is not needed to light a tall tree's trunk or canopy.

Teaching Via the Intensive Course **International Landscape Lighting Institute**

Saluki Park Mockup Areas – Lighting the Black Walnuts

Above left, you see a Platanus ocidentalis/American Sycamore, distant right, and Morus alba/White Mulberry, distant left. The team that lit the Mulberry lit the all the canopy's width, but not the Walnuts or the Sycamore. Above right, the LRC students that lit the Norway Maple relit the single Black Walnut and now the canopy width can be seen.

In April 2004 Dan Dyer, and I did a mockup trying downlights for the trunk instead of uplighting, as the planting space near the staircase is so tight. The obvious benefit, besides much softer trunk lighting, is that the downlighting covers the stairs and surrounding planting. Interestingly, we reshot the stairs in August and found that the foliage in spring is very light and then darkens into the summer.

After those mockups, the Black Walnut tree trunks got permanently lit using downlight. It provides safe lighting on those uneven stairs and simply looks better overall.

International Landscape Lighting Institute *Teaching Via the Intensive Course*

SECTION IV

Saluki Park Mockup Areas – Lighting the Black Walnuts

Between 2008 and 2012 we did a lot of testing with LED as it was emerging as a viable architectural light source. At first, LED sources did not produce enough candlepower for landscape lighting. After a few years we began asking LED chip manufacturers and landscape lighting fixture manufacturers for less output. One manufacturer, DauerLED (dauermanufacturing.com), released a 2-watt MR16 that is great for small elements in a scene and for lighting tree trunks. The "MR" lamp replacements today have multiple beam spreads up to 60, 80, and even 120°. This really helps landscape lighting, where we typically need wide beam spreads.

We kept testing the lighting effects of lamping on that pair of Black Walnuts flanking the stairs. The top right photo shows the lighting with only the original halogen (incandescent) on both trees. It is beautiful but with multiple fixtures per tree, using incandescent means that the wattage load is high.

On the eve of the 2012 ILLI Intensive Course, I wanted to light the right tree with LED as a comparison with halogen (still on the left). I ordered some Soraa 9.5 watt lamps (they started at 12.5 and continually lowered the output settling at 7.5 later) in 2700°K. When they arrived, we installed them in the tree, photo above left. What we saw really surprised me. The wattage was only 9.5 watts compared with a combination of 35 and 50-watt halogen and the LED candlepower output was significantly lower. The lighting effect on the right tree, you can see is a much higher light level. It took me awhile to understand that and I believe it has to do with multiple LED chips all sending the light primarily forward so more candlepower is directed straight ahead. The other surprise though, is that the 2700°K color really doesn't look good on the foliage of that right tree.

I called Soraa asking for 3000° kelvin lamps to be shipped overnight, as the class was starting the next day. When the lamps arrived, upper right photo, you see it looks great and it still brighter than the halogen, at about 70% reduction in wattage consumption. However, the 3000° lamps only lasted a year, even though the fixtures were not used much and should not have failed. We replaced those with the new 7.5 watts lamps, which had significantly less output, and a year later I noticed that the color looked different and the output had decreased significantly. Studying these new LED, George was photographing all the lamps sent to us for ILLI. We had hundreds of photos, including the 7.5 watt lamp put in to replace the failed 9.5, (on the next page, lower left). To the right is a photo above, George took over that same lamp after one year. Notice the color shift and decrease in output. Even today, I am not clear that lamp degradation in both output and color shift is not still a problem with LED lamps.

Teaching Via the Intensive Course   International Landscape Lighting Institute
SECTION IV

Saluki Park Mockup Areas – Lighting the Black Walnuts

International Landscape Lighting Institute *Teaching Via the Intensive Course*
SECTION IV

Saluki Park Mockup Areas – Lighting the Black Walnuts

On the individual Black Walnut on the lower lawn, prior to LED, we tested halogen in both left photos and used metal halide in the right photos. You can see a big color difference, between the warmer halogen and the cooler metal halide, both during dormancy and when the trees are in-leaf. You can see that the selection of light source makes no difference in lighting a tree – you can light a tree, or anything in landscape, with any light source. What does make a difference is the color of light that radiates from a light source and how it appears on that object.

Saluki Park Mockup Areas – Lighting the Black Walnuts

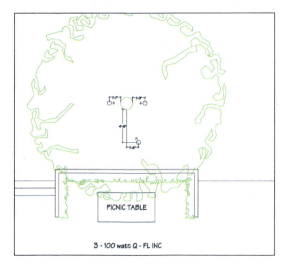

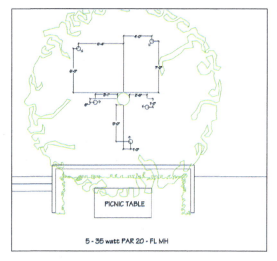

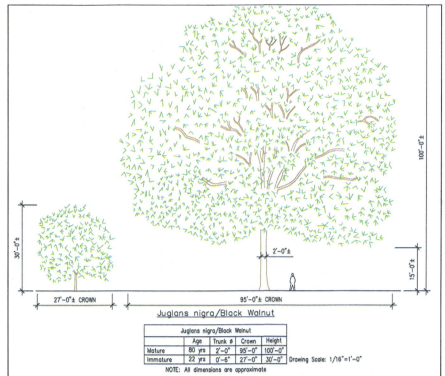

For this comparison, we also compared the number of fixtures needed and the wattage consumed. On this page, the upper drawings show that the halogen (left) uses three 100-watt, 120 volt fixtures; while the metal halide (right) required six 35-watt lamps equaling 210 watts, before 'ballast loss' or the energy consumed by that voltage limiting device. The energy use of the ballast is usually around 15%, adding about 32 watts, which means it still uses less than the incandescent. If the lamps were low voltage halogen or LED, both would consume less wattage: using 5 x 35 watts low voltage is only 175 watts while 5 x 7.5 watts is 37.5 watts. Both the low voltage halogen or LED will be much smaller physically, easier to integrate into a landscape with minimal visual impact. We also need to consider lamp life. Traditional 120-volt incandescent lamps have very short lamp life; a negative when selecting a light source; metal halide varies between 6,000 – 15,000 hours. Incandescent lamps can be under-voltaged by reducing the voltage setting on the transformer or dimming, making a low voltage MR16 lamp with a 6,000 hour life exponentially increase its life to around 27,000 hours. LED lamp manufacturers list their lamp's life between 25,000 – 50,000, but lamp degradation and actual life still suggest that, today in 2021, we cannot rely on such high numbers.

International Landscape Lighting Institute *Teaching Via the Intensive Course*
SECTION IV

Saluki Park Mockup Areas – Lighting Individual Conifers

These five images show four different teams' lighting on the same Picea pungens/Colorado Blue Spruce at the north end of the pond, near both Jan's and George's studios. This tree was lit most years. It branches to the ground, requiring all fixtures be located outside the canopy. Between 70–80 years old, it reaches 75'/23m high with at least a 20'/6m width.

Many trees light well, and this is a great example of that. Almost any approach you take works , as long as you place fixtures close enough to the tree to graze it up its outer edges, or move back far enough to wash it, as the 1999 team did using fixtures from two sides with the flood lighting the bottom two thirds of the tree and the spot lighting the very top. Look closely and you can see the difference, but, normally, it is just looks nicely covered from top to bottom.

This daytime image shows Spruce boughs are each long and textured.

This 1999 LRC team used two metal halide lamps: one spot for the top from the left side and one flood from the right.

The 2003 LRC team, later, used multiple MR16 halogen lamps all around the tree increasing its three dimensions.

In 2007 ILLI designers chose to graze two sides to the emphasize structure and texture on the tree.

This 2008 team lit the boughs with multiple 50-watt MR16 fixtures from one side only.

Teaching Via the Intensive Course **International Landscape Lighting Institute**

Saluki Park Mockup Areas – Lighting Individual Conifers

Along the studio driveway hillside, this Abies/Fir species has long boughs but a more open form than the spruce, so the 2008 team put fixtures inside the canopy to show the trunks, with others of their fixtures literally down the hillside aiming up to create the grazing all the way to the top.

Near the south end of the pond these Wichita Junipers were typically gently washed as part of a group (left). This Chamaecyparis obtusa /False Cypress species (right), 2014, is washed from two sides at about 45° off center of the tree as a focal point.

International Landscape Lighting Institute *Teaching Via the Intensive Course*
SECTION IV

Saluki Park Mockup Areas – Lighting the Beech Trees

These photos show the American Beech and, at top, the baby Camperdown Elm after being just planted in 2006. The Beech has multiple branches and doesn't respond well to pruning, so we tried to limit that. Having a majestic form, it was lit over and over, so we will see multiple lighting approaches in the next few pages. In 2014, lower right on the next page, the trunk structure is uplit from the ground helping to bring yours eyes to the ground in the overall composition.

Teaching Via the Intensive Course **International Landscape Lighting Institute**
SECTION IV

Saluki Park Mockup Areas – Lighting the Beech Trees

Above, the Camperdown Elm has grown up a lot from that upper left page photo. It was a challenge for many groups. On page 273, we saw it uplit from the outside, while here, even after David's pruning or because of it, the team left it in silhouette by lighting the three kinds of Sorbaria/False Spirea behind it. Lighting all that ground plane planting and the other two trees, using splashes of strong light on the lower structure, created the effect of holding your eye at, human scale, leading you towards the new path to the remote parking area. Inserting strong splashes of light throughout the canopy adds to creating an overall appearance for the tree.

International Landscape Lighting Institute *Teaching Via the Intensive Course*
SECTION IV

Saluki Park Mockup Areas – Lighting the Beech Trees

Lighting this Beech has always required lighting the bigger specimens around it, whether in 2006 top, 2010 above, or the other two scenes on the next page, as we saw on pages 254 and 255. Each team approached the overall tree, wrestling with that very difficult branching structure. Some lit the tree to be more dramatic or the focal point, even though it is not as massive as either of the trees flanking it. Some teams integrated the trunk structure with the canopy and others highlighted it more than the canopy. This shows how multiple design groups can have very differing approaches and all be successful – careful fixture placement, aiming, and shielding, in all cases, stop you from seeing fixture brightness which would visually disrupt any of these scenes.

Saluki Park Mockup Areas – Lighting the Beech Trees

In both lower photos, on both pages, teams ventured into lighting the background behind the Beech leaving the canopy softly lit. The bottom photo, on the previous page, the stronger light on the Evergreens in the back, helped define the Beech's form. Lighting the massing of low plantings (photo immediately above), the 2011 team has all the elements act as an overall scene, rather than creating a hierarchy with the Beech being prominent. The 2008 team (above top photo) accomplished a similar goal, but increased the lighting level on all the trees including the False Cypress shrubs in the mid background, and with everything else around it dark, created a more dramatic, almost theatrical scene.

International Landscape Lighting Institute *Teaching Via the Intensive Course*
SECTION IV

Saluki Park Mockup Areas – Lighting the Beech Trees

Teaching Via the Intensive Course **International Landscape Lighting Institute**

Saluki Park Mockup Areas – Lighting the Beech Trees

This Beech tree is an example of a very difficult tree to light. In these photos, you see the complicated and tight branching structure. Some teams used brighter light, others softer, and it is a designer's prerogative to make these decisions with the client's agreement. The closeup of the structure, left page, upper right with both up and downlighting softly and evenly shows the form in 2010. Next to that, on the previous page, top left in 2002, using more brightness variation across the canopy and on the trunk, the designer makes the tree a strong focal point, in a mysterious, dramatic setting. Above, 2014, and lower left, 2006, both teams make the heavy canopy appear light and airy with small variation of brightness contrast across it's width.

Growing typically to 80'/24m wide, this tree was between 80–90 years old over the years we lit it for the classes. Having a dense canopy, and, early in our mockup timeframe, that upright, oval crown, which will eventually spread out to a soft dome, the way teams needed to approach it changed from the early years to the later years. This kind of change, while very subtle in this case, requires the owner, with the designer and the maintenance team, to reevaluate the lighting over time. Early projects I suggest reviews annually, unless it is a newly planted landscape, then maybe a couple of times the first year. For established projects, where change typically occurs more slowly, reviews can be several years, unless the client is fastidious about the appearance of the landscape, then more frequent visits keep the gardens looking more perfect.

International Landscape Lighting Institute *Teaching Via the Intensive Course*
SECTION IV

Saluki Park Mockup Areas – Lighting the Apple Orchard

Our Apple orchard was planted in the 1920s. Many Apple trees had perished, leaving space for me to add some Maples for fall color. In the top photo, the 2007 team moved furniture into their scene. At top right, on the next page, multiple uplights, placed close to the trunk reveals the tree's texture, shows the overall branching structure, and the width of the canopy. Because the branching and leaf overlap of apples can be dense without annual pruning, the light doesn't penetrate the canopy all the way to the top.

Teaching Via the Intensive Course **International Landscape Lighting Institute**

Saluki Park Mockup Areas – Lighting the Apple Orchard

In all these photos, the design teams use tree mount downlights to show the ground plane. At lower left, on the previous page, the 2009 team lit the upper pathway shining through the branches to create patterns, as did the 2010 team (lower photo, above) on the ground, helping integrate the tree into the scene. The 2007 team (upper photo, above) uses that downlighting to connect between trees, providing visual cohesion.

International Landscape Lighting Institute *Teaching Via the Intensive Course*
SECTION IV

Saluki Park Mockup Areas – Lighting the Apple Orchard

Three Apple trees, above, seem to be the focal area in this scene. The 2014 team lit across the canopies with undulating brightness level and used both up and downlighting to sculpt the multi-trunk branching structure as a sculptural element. Looking closely at the far left tree (above), you can see the light layering they used on the trunks, highlighting areas, and sweeps of downlight below the tree and across the lawn beyond. By the end of the class, they leave out the Oak behind the Apples and inserted the heron, seen previously at the pond, using saturated blue so the bird stands up

Teaching Via the Intensive Course **International Landscape Lighting Institute**

Saluki Park Mockup Areas – Lighting the Apple Orchard

to the maple (whose vivid color, always fleeting, has already started to fade). To complete the scene, they have gently lit the shrubs beyond the orchard. In the overall photo (above), you can see that it kept the sculpting effects, but softened the Apple Trees, shifting the emphasis to the sculpture during all seasons, and letting the Maples take center stage during those few weeks of glory in fall as they go dormant.

International Landscape Lighting Institute *Teaching Via the Intensive Course*
SECTION IV

Saluki Park Mockup Areas – Lighting the Oaks and Maples

This Quercus rubra/Red Oak sits back in the north entrance to the central forest, almost unseen, until it gets lit. This 2006 team caresses the trunk, using two uplights on the left and right sides, and multiple uplights that create a glorious statement across the canopies width and to it's top. Surrounding shrubs and trees they lit slightly softer so this tree is the star.

Teaching Via the Intensive Course **International Landscape Lighting Institute**

SECTION IV

Saluki Park Mockup Areas – Lighting the Oaks and Maples

Mentioned earlier, this 2009 ILLI team became the first at to light a tree entirely with LED. It was so early in developing LED fixtures for landscape lighting that the team had to use fixtures from multiple manufacturers: some traditional fixtures with LED drop-in lamps, others with integral modules, some having multiple optic options and dimming at the fixture – this development gave us field flexibility we hadn't previously had. This photo is from the back side showing all the brightness that the angled glare shields prevent from normal viewing angles. Note that the canopy top is dark.

International Landscape Lighting Institute *Teaching Via the Intensive Course*
SECTION IV

Saluki Park Mockup Areas – Lighting the Oaks and Maples

In October 2014, this Acer saccharum/Sugar Maple, located in the southern boundary border and normally not even noticed, became a star in its 90s. This tree can live 400 years, so even though it is over 70'/21+m high, it will continue to grow. This ILLI team uplights the canopy front from the right side, letting other parts fade into the night and, with one tree mount fixture, softly reveals the trunk and bark's texture, visually connecting the tree to the ground.

Teaching Via the Intensive Course **International Landscape Lighting Institute**

Saluki Park Mockup Areas – Lighting the Oaks and Maples

The 1999 LRC students were the first to light this Acer platinoides/Norway Maple, with their mockup staying up for a year. They have multiple stake mount uplights laid out on the ground, covering the width of this over 50'/15m. Uplights, mounted 3/4 to the top, provide light at the crown due to massive leaves and dense leaf overlap that prohibits uplighting reaching the top from fixtures at the ground. Our big surprise was the spring appearance in full bloom – no one thinks of Maple trees flowers.

International Landscape Lighting Institute *Teaching Via the Intensive Course*
SECTION IV
Saluki Park Mockup Areas – Lighting the Oaks and Maples

This Acer platinoides/Norway Maple lit many times over the years, for this early October 2008 team, still had a green canopy. This tree tends to change color later in the fall (on the far left canopy side, signs of color are starting to show). They lit the tree from the ground, both under and outside the canopy. The undulation of brightness across the canopy, and nearly to/through the crown creates a strong sculptural effect.

Over ten years after the first team, this tree has grown substantially, and while the first lighting revealed the branching structure into the canopy, when dormant in winter with snow and then with spring flowers, the structure has now opened up, allowing the structure to show while in-leaf.

This team's approach included lighting smaller plantings on the left and right extending the scene, with this big tree treated as the star. In addition, the team used a little downlighting to show the trunk and provide connection to the ground. The three areas of ground plane lighting provide cohesion across the landscape while still letting the tree shine as the focal point.

Their approach is still rather theatrically dramatic compared to the 2012 team, right page.

Teaching Via the Intensive Course   **International Landscape Lighting Institute**

Saluki Park Mockup Areas – Lighting the Oaks and Maples

Teams saw what previous teams did in their areas only after they had started their design. I waited until the third day to teach tree lighting, so that teams were not impacted by previous designs. This 2012 team incorporated more plantings surrounding the maple, and late October that year enjoyed the most spectacular fall color the tree had ever experienced. The team lit the trees and plantings on both sides while carefully crafting the light level variations so that the tree, while towering over everything around it, still serves as the focal point of the scene.

As trees turn color in the fall, their leaves are also falling – this tree's canopy opened more than normal, allowing light from ground mounted fixtures to reach its crown.

This team incorporated more downlighting in addition to the wider scene uplighting, showing under/around the Catalpa speciosa/Northern Catalpa and the gathering area under the Maple canopy. Its canopy is over 50'/15m wide with the branching pruned over the years to about 15'/4.5+m above ground, creating a large outdoor living space that we used all the time.

International Landscape Lighting Institute *Teaching Via the Intensive Course*
SECTION IV
Mockups and Installations – Brunswick, New York

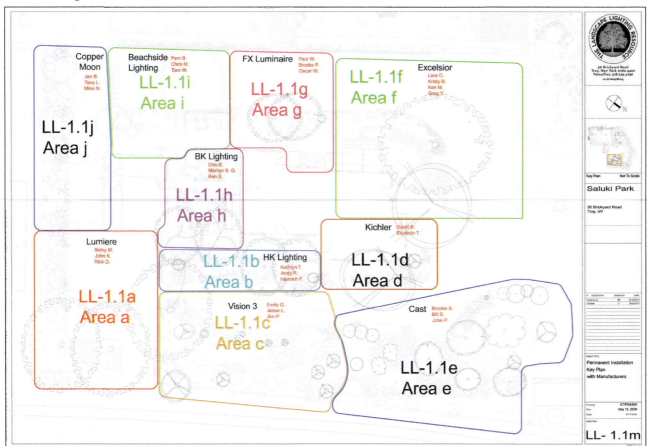

ILLI's first permanent installation site plan (above) shows ten areas designed by teams using one manufacturer's equipment. Designed and installed in two sessions, the installation session included power distribution demonstrations.

304

Teaching Via the Intensive Course **International Landscape Lighting Institute**

Mockups and Installations – Brunswick, New York

Never hindered, our teams made glare shields as needed. Different from the mockup classes, these permanent installations showed our designers and mentors parts of the lighting process that they may not have otherwise experienced. Showing designers what installers know, and vice versa – this integration of knowledge across the entire process of lighting benefits all team members.

International Landscape Lighting Institute *Teaching Via the Intensive Course*
SECTION IV

Mockups and Installations – Brunswick, New York

Power distribution is a fundamental requirement for landscape lighting. Some properties will have power throughout, but many don't. Providing distribution throughout is easy when a property is initially under construction. For a 6-acre property like Saluki Park, developed in the 1920s with no power distribution, demonstrating a slick technique to extend power from the source at the garage to a remote tractor barn 400 '/122m away, showed that it is complicated and takes the entire team to get it done.

Using a vacuum, a cable is pulled through the conduit (at top), and through a curve in the pipe to the other end. Below left, a trench had to be dug to locate the conduit. Lower right, the pipes are connected using water-resistant adhesive. Notice that below the pipe are exposed roots that our arborist used an air-gun to get beneath, allowing us to not cut through major roots.

The upper left photo on the next page shows several of us holding multiple cables while being pulled through the pipe to the remote equipment barn supplying all the needs for this project and other/future needs.

Teaching Via the Intensive Course **International Landscape Lighting Institute**

Mockups and Installations – Brunswick, New York

We held the cables as lubrication was added, enabling the multiple cables to move through the conduit. A team at the shed end pulled on the cables as we steadied them at the origination end. Looking at equipment outside and inside the shed (the lower middle and right photos), you would never know all the effort it took to move multiple 120-volt lines extending our power capacity.

The entire project took over a year to plan, prepare, and execute. Teams prepared design drawings and specifications which ILLI used to prepare formal contract documents for each of the ten areas and order all the equipment for the fall installation, which was integrated into the final record Ddocuments for maintenance and educational tours (see pages 318 and 319). Having both traditional halogen, new layouts in LED, and one area still incandescent, allowed complete comparisons between old and new technologies. Unlike the mockups, turned off on the final night so all the lighting was gone, this lighting remained to show public groups and future classes.

International Landscape Lighting Institute *Teaching Via the Intensive Course*
SECTION IV
Mockups and Installations – Brunswick, New York

Arborists from multiple firms, including Bartlett Tree Care (bartlett.com) spent many daylight and night hours installing fixtures in trees for the teams.

In Area E, Cast Lighting fixtures (cast-lighting.com) with an LED integral module dimmed at each fixture and multiple optics options, were used, (see pages 314 and 315). In the photo, at bottom, the mounting canopy can be set at an angle in the tree providing aiming flexibility.

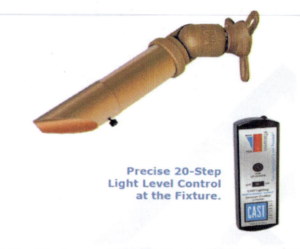

Precise 20-Step Light Level Control at the Fixture.

LED Light Source: (1) Cree LED, Est. Life (L70) 42,300 hrs., 2,700° K, 80 CRI

Input Voltage: 10 to 24 V, AC or DC

Power: 4.9 W, 0.7 pf, 7.0 VA

Lumen Output: 299 lm (LED), 253 lm (luminaire with 64° Optics

Choice of (5) easy-to-replace optics, including extremly narrow (13°), narrow (24°), medium (40°), wide (64°) (comes with fixture), and assymetric (15° x 39°).*

Teaching Via the Intensive Course **International Landscape Lighting Institute**

SECTION IV

Mockups and Installations – Brunswick, New York

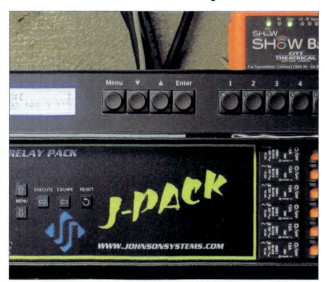

Situated in the basement of the house, the Cue Server processor sits on top of the J-PACK switching module. The SHOW Baby is the RF communications link to the garage.

The DP-415 is an additional switching module for handling more loads.

Don Bradley installing the other J-PACK switching module in the garage.

Eric Beaudin, the donor of this equipment, is documenting the installation.

The individual fixture dimming, that several companies provided including BK Lighting, bklighting.com (the first to offer it), Cast Lighting, (cast-lighting.com), FX Luminaire, (fx.com), and HK Lighting Group, (hklightinggroup.com), allows setting lighting levels throughout a scene before being affected by the overall control system (donated by Eric Beaudin, Aquasol Solutions, info@solutionsaquasol.com).

Having this control system allows us to control all ten areas individually, including all of the zones in each area. We programmed it to have each area come on zone by zone over time, and when a section included more than manufacturer and design teams' area, we can have one area come on followed by another until that entire area is lit.

This allows having tours to show interested parties the opportunities that landscape lighting offers. Seeing good lighting helps people understand what can be done, and by seeing multiple types of lighting helps them decide what they would like to have at their own property.

This control system had equipment located in multiple locations and we had it controlled by phone and tablets so that we could cue the varying options in the field with the tours visiting the property.

International Landscape Lighting Institute *Teaching Via the Intensive Course*
SECTION IV
Mockups and Installations – Brunswick, New York

Above, a tour is being conducted by a mentor, with a new ILLI Intensive Course class on the first night. We started integrating tours of the Landscape Lighting Exhibition after the first day and night's sessions to leave the attendees with amazing visions of these ten areas surrounding the main house while they got much-needed sleep on their first night of the five-day course.

The upper image on the right page, Area A, the manufacturer is Lumiere, Cooper Lighting Solutions (cooperlighting.com) shows the arrival drive area. This team used Lumiere tree mounted fixtures to downlight the parking and the entry gate area, providing access to the front yard. The fixtures uplight several mature trees surrounding the arrival/parking area. The design had to include the neon-backed Saluki sculpture in the peak above the garage door, which set the lighting levels and acts as the focal point, drawing guests into the area.

Below that image is a view back to the drive area from Area B, showing the downlighting on the gate and how it integrates seamlessly with Area B. This area has HK Lighting Group (hklightinggroup.com) as its manufacturer. The Area B team coordinated in this corner with Area C, including this downlighting on the sidewalk from their Red Oak tree – the branches hanging over the path would have been dark without the downlighting creating those patterns on the walkway.

Area B has four Magnolia soulangeana/Saucer Magnolia trees in a line from the driveway to the front door. All are surrounded by hedging, all planted in the 1920s. The designers placed uplights on extension stems into the hedging, at what I call the plants' shoulder, to minimize its appearance and not interfere with the light distribution up into the trees. The canopies on all were large, requiring additional normal stake-mount uplights in planting beds adjacent to the hedges to complete the lighting for the Magnolia canopies. The Magnolias also had downlights for walkways and stairs, along with downlighting the dark-colored foliage of the hedges. The little tree is a young Amelanchier lamarckii/Juneberry and the young hedge behind, Taxus media 'Citation'/ Citation Columnar Yews, are all uplit, with the Yews casting shadows on the dark fencing, for now.

Teaching Via the Intensive Course **International Landscape Lighting Institute**

Mockups and Installations – Brunswick, New York

International Landscape Lighting Institute *Teaching Via the Intensive Course*
SECTION IV
Mockups and Installations – Brunswick, New York

Above are views from Area B to H and below is their opposite. The Juneberry (at left) shows in its uplighting, as do the Magnolias and the lawn Black Walnut, located in Area I in the distance. You can see the downlighting for the paths and stairs from ring- or tree-mount fixtures in the Magnolias.

Teaching Via the Intensive Course International Landscape Lighting Institute

Mockups and Installations – Brunswick, New York

Area B (at top) uses downlighting for the front wall and patios, with up/downlighting on the Acer palmatum 'Bloodgood'/Bloodgood Japanese Maple, (page 156). In Area C above, Vision 3 lighting (vision3lighting.com) downlighting shows multiple Hydrangeas with a young Corylus avellana 'Contorta'/Contorted Hazlenut and two Thuja occidentalis 'Spiralis'/Spiralis Eastern Arborvitae uplit as focal points. This is the area that remained halogen/incandescent. Looking around these four photos, without being told, it would be difficult to identify what lighting remained halogen and those that were changed to LED.

International Landscape Lighting Institute *Teaching Via the Intensive Course*
SECTION IV
Mockups and Installations – Brunswick, New York

Looking both directions through the front gardens encompasses four areas: B, C, D, and E. The designers integrated all four areas into one design brilliantly, taking advantage of the sculpture, specimen plants, and views from all the living spaces out into the gardens. At the north end of the view, the Euyonomous alata/Burning Bush, provides a colorful background for the sculpture.

Teaching Via the Intensive Course **International Landscape Lighting Institute**

Mockups and Installations – Brunswick, New York

In Area D (top), Kichler (kichler.com), the designers, downlit the PJM Rhododendrons outside the living room windows. Above, in Area E , Cast (cast-lighting.com) provides the up/downlighting of the anchor tree, Enkianthus campanulatus/ Redvein Enkianthus. Landscape/lighting plans for this area are shown on pages 318 and 319, showing the detail into which each team went to prepare their designs.

International Landscape Lighting Institute *Teaching Via the Intensive Course*
SECTION IV

Mockups and Installations – Brunswick, New York

Area F, Excelsior Lighting (excelsriorlighting.com) just off the north end, has master bedroom windows and the sleeping porch (complete with dog door). The Black Walnuts (see page 283) are on one end, and the Sycamore (above), now well lit with both up and downlighting for the tree, the guest bedroom patio, and surrounds – it gives you the feeling of being in a tree house surrounded by night beauty.

Teaching Via the Intensive Course   **International Landscape Lighting Institute**

Mockups and Installations – Brunswick, New York

Above photos show areas F, G, H, I, and J, lighting along the back of the home. Black Walnuts loose their leaves early, while the Apple and Oaks still hold theirs. In Area I, Beachside Lighting (beachsidelighting.com) designers use framing projectors that create patterns on the lawn, downlight foundation plantings at the base of the raised patio, and highlight the star on the back of the garden shed.

International Landscape Lighting Institute *Teaching Via the Intensive Course*
SECTION IV

Mockups and Installations – Brunswick, New York

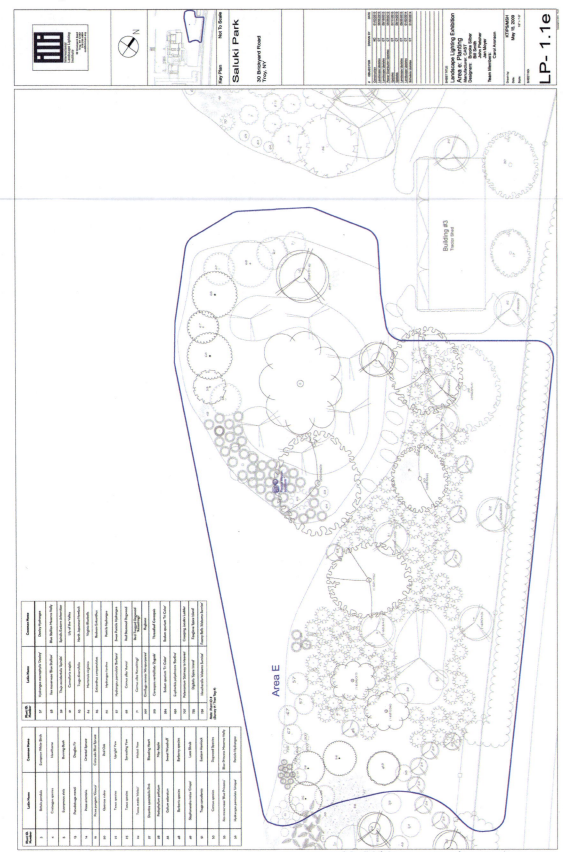

Teaching Via the Intensive Course **International Landscape Lighting Institute**

SECTION IV

Mockups and Installations – Brunswick, New York

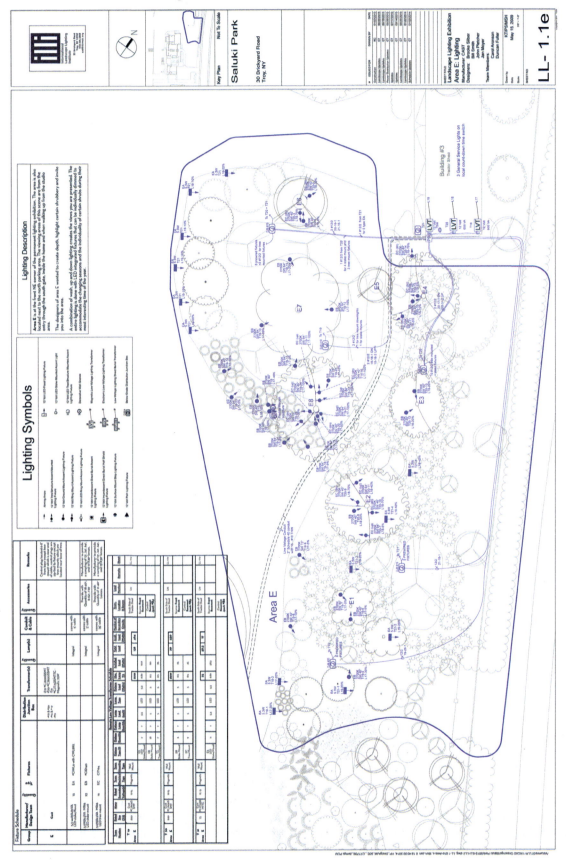

International Landscape Lighting Institute *Teaching Via the Intensive Course*
SECTION IV
Mockups and Installations – Rio Verde, Arizona 2015 & 2019

In 2015 and 2019, ILLI held Intensive Courses at Rio Verde, AZ, designing and installing a permanent installation initially, and then providing maintenance and growth suggestions for the park adjacent to the Community Building and Country Club. Three attendee teams with mentors and two mentor teams tackled lighting this Sonoran Desert park, designing and installing in a week during the first class, and then servicing that design and preparing expansion ideas; essentially tackling how much the new plants from 2015 had grown. Both sessions elevated both attendees' and mentors' experiences and expanded their project skills.

Teaching Via the Intensive Course **International Landscape Lighting Institute**

SECTION IV

Mockups and Installations – Rio Verde, Arizona 2015 & 2019

In the Sonoran Desert the light/dark cycle stays nearly the same all year, so it is dark relatively early all year. Grazing Carnegiea gigantea/Saguaro and Fouquieria splendens/Ocotillo shows their form, bringing their textures to life. A grouping of Cercidium microphyllum/Foothills Palo Verde trees have soft uplighting. They are typically green multi-trunk trees with very small leaves.

International Landscape Lighting Institute *Teaching Via the Intensive Course*
SECTION IV
Mockups and Installations – Rio Verde, Arizona 2015 & 2019

Another desert native, the Opuntia cactus (above in back) has multiple species. This one is uplit from outside and a fixture inserted into the clump. Several large mature trees, lit by the mentor teams, have both up and downlighting. Rio Verde residents have gathered for the last night reveal.

Teaching Via the Intensive Course **International Landscape Lighting Institute**

Mockups and Installations – Rio Verde, Arizona 2015 & 2019

Many people attend the last night reveals. In Rio Verde in 2015 one of the largest number of residents of any event in the neighborhood chose to attend this reveal. One of the issues the teams faced here is clearly evident in the lower photo: the parking lot lights are very bright, nearly overshadowing the softer landscape light. The very large Mesquite from the genus Prosopis, at the far end of the park, has a graceful form. The team uplit it, showing the entire canopy and downlit around it.

International Landscape Lighting Institute *Teaching Via the Intensive Course*
SECTION IV
Mockups and Installations – Rio Verde, Arizona 2015 & 2019

In the upper photo, during daylight, Jesse Loucks, an ILLI mentor lighting designer trained to climb, changes a lamp in this Mesquite in 2019. A very large mature specimen, it towers over the entrance to the park on the way to the RV Clubhouse. In the lower right photo, you see the Mesquite in context of the park. The teams used Teka path lights (tekaillumination.com) along the newly developed and planted park in 2015, and lit varying plants within the park. It is seen from streets on three sides and the parking lot on the fourth side. This makes controlling fixture brightness very difficult. Most path lights have some lens brightness showing. In a park setting, using pathlights or bollards may become necessary for people to traverse the site safely, when downlighting locations don't exist.

Teaching Via the Intensive Course **International Landscape Lighting Institute**

Mockups and Installations – Rio Verde, Arizona 2015 & 2019

This project, the first public ILLI site, introduces issues similar to residential sites, but on a different scale. Rio Verde is a 55+ community with an aging population. Walkways, like the one in the upper left photo, (2019), need to be lit to a higher, more even light level for aging eyes. The fixtures to light this pathway are located in the trellis above the outdoor dining patio.

The Mesquite in the upper right photo, I lit in the years between the initial 2015 installation and the 2019 class. I used below-grade fixtures all around the tree to hide the fixtures and multiple small ring-mount fixtures installed in the canopy to light the pathway from the Community Center. This one tree was expanded in 2019 along the median, with that lighting permanently installed in 2021. Viewed from the club dining patio, note how the trunk form and texture is revealed.

Palm trees aren't native to the Sonoran Desert, but many are used throughout the Phoenix basin. The 2019 teams lit this one with the Palo Verde trees through the path in the median along a street connecting the club and the Community Center (lower left). The lower right photo shows Agaves being up/downlit, uplighting on Palo Verde trees, and downlighting for the path and a large clump of Opuntia. This photo shows the street lights used throughout the community. They have a wide spread, using High Pressure Sodium, that golden light many streets use in the USA. These, however, have no direct view of the lamp that we saw in the parking lot lights. Even though you see the fixture's brightness, it is not as strong. Changing from any HID source to LED has been a challenge for most street light fixtures as most still produce too much fixture brightness.

International Landscape Lighting Institute *Teaching Via the Intensive Course*

SECTION IV

Mockups and Installations – Ridgewood, New Jersey 2016

In 2016, ILLI needed a class site. During my transition from New York to Arizona, Brooke Silber and I had formed a partnership. Brooke had landed a park project in Ridgewood, NJ and they agreed to become an ILLI permanent installation site. This is the poster George made to send out inviting the community to attend the unveiling of the lighting for their park.

Teaching Via the Intensive Course   International Landscape Lighting Institute
SECTION IV

Mockups and Installations – Ridgewood, New Jersey 2016

The park is a square in the center of town surrounded on four sides by businesses and shops. The site is raised above street level on several sides, with stairs from the main street to access the park. As you can see on the poster on the previous page, there is parking around it on all four sides.

As with most parks, throughout are commemorative plaques and sculptures noting the town's history. The path system includes a central circle that has booths set up during the summer for multiple types of events.

Unlike most ILLI projects, this one had guidelines, developed with the town, that the lighting teams needed to work with, so they didn't have free reign as they do for other courses, even other permanent installations.

One more thing from the poster. Note that the lighting reveal gathering point has been identified. The teams work together to determine how the audience will move through the site for the presentations. Logistics always need attention. While not strictly lighting, designers need to think about all the aspects of a project beyond just their lighting concerns.

In the photo above right, you can see that this team planned multiple fixtures mounted in this tree. With so much activity going on in the park, limiting fixtures at ground level becomes necessary. This drawing notes the fixture type, location, and aiming.

The plan below, for a different team, documents the layout and fixture type. Spreadsheets in another section of the contract/record documents spells out the fixture specification and the lamps required to create the lighting effects.

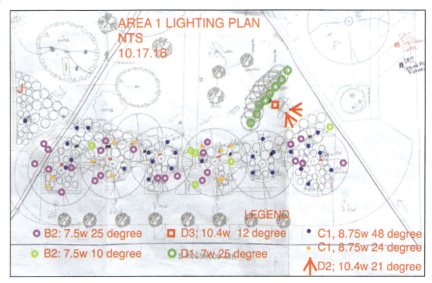

International Landscape Lighting Institute *Teaching Via the Intensive Course*
SECTION IV
Mockups and Installations – Ridgewood, New Jersey 2016

For this project, ILLI held a sponsor roundtable event on the last morning of the class. Each manufacturer sponsor, here owner David Beausoleil, Cast Lighting (cast-lighting.com), got to meet with all the attendees and mentors to show their fixtures, while building relationships with designers from throughout the USA and the world.

The lower photos shows daytime and night work installing and aiming fixtures in trees. In this case, the arborists used lift trucks. Paving throughout the park handles the weight of these machines and makes both installation and aiming easier and quicker.

Teaching Via the Intensive Course **International Landscape Lighting Institute**
SECTION IV

Mockups and Installations – Ridgewood, New Jersey 016

At top, you see the lighting of the main entry with overall downlighting covering plantings, the stairs, and the wall seat. In another area of the park, trees around the bench are lit, along with the commemorative plaque. While this bench has some light, the designers kept most light off the bench so people are not on display.

International Landscape Lighting Institute *Teaching Via the Intensive Course*
SECTION IV
Mockups and Installations – Ridgewood, New Jersey 2016

Along the main street, globe street lights produce a lot of brightness that the teams have to take into account. The row of trees are lit to a light level that allows the park lighting to integrate with the street lighting, but without fixture brightness. Then as you move into the park, away from the brighter street lighting, the light levels can step down to softer levels. Within hours of the lighting being turned on that first night, groups of people started gathering in the park.

An ILLI sponsor, manufacturer Attraction Lights (attractionlights.com), produced a custom bollard with the park name on it to use along the circle path in the cent of the park. With, 'Van Neste Square', cut into the bollard, intriguing light patterns surround each bollard.

The sculpture (right page) commemorates townspeople who served the community. The names are on the plaques at the base. To light this, the teams needed both tree-mounted fixtures to show the US eagle at the top.

Teaching Via the Intensive Course   **International Landscape Lighting Institute**
SECTION IV

Mockups and Installations – Ridgewood, New Jersey 2016

They chose to light the bird with a contrasting color light from the plinth. Coming from multiple angles, they show the bird's form and feathering texture. Uplighting on the plinth shows the patterning and the column top. Downlighting covers the base with the plaques and the surrounding area, providing context for the park's important feature .

International Landscape Lighting Institute *Teaching Via the Intensive Course*
SECTION IV
Mockups and Installations – Tokamachi, Japan 2017

Hiroshi Kira of HK Lighting called me one day in 2016 to inquire if ILLI would consider doing a course in his home town, Tokamachi, Japan. Logistics of holding a course in a country half way around the planet, with a language barrier, was worked out in a series of meetings in Tokamachi. The site, Kiyotsugawa Fresh Park, situated along the Kiyotsugawa River, offered a unique experience for an ILLI class. Above, Tokamachi City Mayor Yoshifumi Sekiguchi, thanks Hiroshi for the gift to the city. Below, on the left side of the aerial photo you can see the park.

Teaching Via the Intensive Course   **International Landscape Lighting Institute**

SECTION IV

Mockups and Installations – Tokamachi, Japan 2017

Some of the logistics included where the attendees and mentors would stay and how to feed them. Residents volunteered to fix three meals a day for all – attendees, mentors, instructors, and sponsors – at the building above: the town community center. On the upper level of the building, meals and all lectures occurred.

Everyone gathered here multiple times a day – a short walk from the park. At night everyone was transported to another area with several buildings offering traditional Japanese sleeping arrangements: women in one building and men in another. Everyone slept on mats, showered and had all their belongings safely stored in their new home.

International Landscape Lighting Institute *Teaching Via the Intensive Course*
SECTION IV
Mockups and Installations – Tokamachi, Japan 2017

The community center first level has the kitchen where community members prepared the meals and brought them upstairs for us to eat in traditional Japanese style. By the end of the week, we were all used to sitting on the floor for both meals and lectures.

Dozens of Tokamachi residents donated their time to feed us and to help with all phases of installation. They brought us multiple tents with tables for all the equipment to be organized and for demonstrations of wiring and connections techniques; teams helped dig trenches for power distribution and additional power extension as the design developed. They brought snacks and drinks out to the site and the park supervisor, Toshiaki Takahashi, serenaded us on his guitar during the frenetic final preparations of the last afternoon, leading up to the lighting reveal to the town residents. The city provided three interpreters from the City International Relations group (from around the world) for the entire class – they took turns interpreting, night and day.

HK Lighting sponsored the entire event, financing bringing all the lecturers and mentors from the United States; two translators, Japanese National, Satoshi Suzuki from their company, and Joshua Frydman, Assistant Professor of Japanese at the OU Department of Modern Languages; all the lighting equipment for the park lighting; all the wiring and tools needed for all teams, including multiple cordless drills and heat guns for waterproofing electrical connections – essentially everything that we used – including shipping ILLI tool boxes for the design teams. Two organizations in Japan, The Japanese Lighting Coordinate Association and the Japanese representatives for HK Lighting supported preparations prior to the course including, procuring all the equipment not coming from the United States.

The park had public restrooms and a covered structure with heated water for soaking your feet while you watched the river. A truly Japanese amenity. The lower photo, next page, shows our Japanese partner in making this course happen, Noburu Eguchi, the former City Regional Manager. The best thing about this experience was the friendships we made, in spite of little to no direct talking with each other, as we didn't know each others language.

Teaching Via the Intensive Course   **International Landscape Lighting Institute**

SECTION IV

Mockups and Installations – Tokamachi, Japan 2017

The images above show lighting equipment arriving at the site; tools being organized for the design teams on a table for pickup to go to their sites; Hiroshi with mentors assembling fixtures for the design teams; and mentors demonstrating how to make electrical connections to our required standards. Our normal Intensive Course exhausts everyone, and this course took effort to a much higher level.

As with traditions in the US, just up the hill at the site was an ice cream vendor, with an amazing view of the river and much more. Coffee, though, was always available at the snack table under a tent, the Japanese planned and manned for us the entire course. We fell in love with Japan and Tokamachi residents.

International Landscape Lighting Institute *Teaching Via the Intensive Course*
SECTION IV
Mockups and Installations – Tokamachi, Japan 2017

It isn't unusual to find mentors in trees at the ILLI, IC course, or to find mentors guiding their teams in ongoing meetings through the design days; what was unusual was the response of the citizens of Tokamach – farmers who left their fields to help, no matter what the site need was this time.

And, also as usual, finally the last night arrives. Tokamachi is a northern city near ski resorts, in the Niigata Prefecture. The plants varied from those we are used to, which happens on many projects, but lighting composition doesn't change.

Teaching Via the Intensive Course **International Landscape Lighting Institute**
SECTION IV

Mockups and Installations – Tokamachi, Japan 2017

Entering the park from the road coming down the hill, upper photo, you see the stream on your right. The teams gently down light the stream area, introducing context for the park. At the end of the pond, several trees are uplit to draw in your eye.

Below, as you continue to move through the park, the designers set up multiple viewing scenes to walk through. Lighting directs your movement on multiple paths through the space, to enjoy all of the park.

International Landscape Lighting Institute *Teaching Via the Intensive Course*
SECTION IV

Mockups and Installations – Tokamachi, Japan 2017

Moving along, you spot the foot-soaking building. It has become a focal point in the night personality the designers create. They provide brush strokes of downlight, again for visual context, and then bring a treasure-trove of trees to life. The overall setting remains dark, as you clearly see in both photos above, respecting the night sky all over our planet.

Teaching Via the Intensive Course   International Landscape Lighting Institute

SECTION IV

Mockups and Installations – Tokamachi, Japan 2017

Multiple views of the foot-soaking building from differing locations throughout the park, with the trees celebrating, bring a contemplative mood to the park after dark.

International Landscape Lighting Institute *Teaching Via the Intensive Course*
SECTION IV
Mockups and Installations – Tokamachi, Japan 2017

Next to the park is an industrial site, but looking at the photos here, you would never know that – on purpose. Light can create whatever you desire, given the site conditions, and, this park had what it needed to reveal a relaxing, intimate place to enjoy the park and the river.

Teaching Via the Intensive Course   International Landscape Lighting Institute

Mockups and Installations – Tokamachi, Japan 2017

Our scope was limited to the park, but Norburu, Hiroshi, and I had long discussed lighting the adjacent waterfall, along the tributary to the side of the river where resident and visiting kids played in the water (during some seasons only). Asked to mock this up before we left, this was my parting gift to Noburu and the city residents.

International Landscape Lighting Institute *Teaching Via the Intensive Course*
SECTION IV
Mockups and Installations – Tokamachi, Japan 2017

The first winter, Tokamachi sent us photographs of the park in an early snow storm. It warmed our hearts that they were able to use the park for portions of the winter. Because of their annual snowfall, residents shovel down to their entry doors from above due to so much snow pack, or have roof entrances for the winter.

Teaching Via the Intensive Course   International Landscape Lighting Institute
SECTION IV

Mockups and Installations – Tokamachi, Japan 2017

With the mentor team standing behind me at the opening festivities, Joelle, our Tokamachi interpreter from San Diego, translated my introductions. You can see, Peeraanong Wongtanakomchai, ILLI mentor from Thailand, raising her hand identifying herself. It truly does take a community to do great things.

International Landscape Lighting Institute *Teaching Via the Intensive Course*
SECTION IV
Mockups and Installations – Tokamachi, Japan 2017

area 4 group

area 5 group

I leave you, my dear readers, with these photos of the proud design groups and their even prouder mentor teams. Please refer to the list of everyone's names, from all classes, in the appendix.

Teaching Via the Intensive Course **International Landscape Lighting Institute**
SECTION IV

Mockups and Installations – ILLI Class Photos

1999 Jonkoping, Sweden

2006 Sydney, Australia

2006 Initial Class as ILLI, Brunswick, NY
Attendees: Don Bradley, John Johansen, Mike Nantz, and Joan Roca, Instructor and Mentor Janet Lennox Moyer

2007 Brunswick, NY
Attendees: Rick Dekeyser, Debra DeMarco, Nathan McCartney, Troy Rankin, Jessica Stanley, Gean Tremaine; Instructors and Mentors: Don Bradley, Janet Lennox Moyer

2008 Class 1 Brunswick, NY
Attendees: Jerry Carter, Larry Iorri, Jesse Loucks, Shannon Markey, Steve O'Conner, Todd Peace, John Pletcher, Jim Ply, Linda Sanford, Bill Smith, Oscar Welch; Instructors and Mentors: Don Bradley, David Brearey, Tom Williams, Janet Lennox Moyer

2008 Class 2 Brunswick, NY
Attendees: Curtis Dennison, Karen Duffy, Yvonne English, Emily Gilmore, Paul Gosselin, Emily Grierson, Meagan McGuire, Tom Pena, Brooke Perin, Mary Ann Rivera, Susan Smith, Paul Welty; Instructors and Mentors: Don Bradley, David Brearey, Tom Williams, Janet Lennox Moyer; Team Support: Jessica Rauscher

2009 Brunswick, NY
Attendees: Gina Calventi, Rosa Capo-Irizarry, Ron Carter, Anna Cheng, Alex Greer, Bob Isleib, Lana Nath, Sara Nonaka, Joe Paton, Bobbi Perry, Gordon Pevzner, John Pletcher, Yayle Roncka, Sally Stoik; IALD Student Attendee: Sara Pletcher; Instructors and Mentors: Don Bradley, David Brearey, Tony Lato, Tom Williams, Janet Lennox Moyer; Team Support: Jessica Rauscher

2010 Brunswick, NY
Attendees: Eric Beaudin, Emily Gorecki, Booth Hemingway, John Kenny, Cory MacCallum, Ken Martin, Jeff Nepple, Allison Schieffelin, Ken Simons, Eduardo Tamayo, Kathryn Toth, Alex Valdez; IALD Student Attendees: Ariel Heintz, Natalia Lesniak, Rita Widjaja; Instructors and Mentors: Don Bradley, David Brearey, Ron Carter, Tony Lato, Pam Morris, John Pletcher, Panitkwan Soontharuck, Tom Williams, Janet Lennox Moyer; Team Support: Lisa Case, Julie Decker, Chef: Debbie Freinberg

International Landscape Lighting Institute *Teaching Via the Intensive Course*

SECTION IV

ILLI Class – Photos Mockups and Installations

2011 Brunswick, NY
Attendees: Darin Ayres, Jeff Crean, Marilyn Goldfine, Rick Gottlieb, Jeff Kamm, Vicki Kohanek, Vickie Lauck, Susan Ljungberg, Tom Marmelstein, Betsy Mitchell, Chris Mitchell, Gerald Schwarzenbach; IALD Student Attendees: Anna Lok, Michael Shepard, Peeraanong Wongtanakomchai; Sponsor: Eric Beaudin, Aquasol Outdoor Lighting; Instructors and Mentors: Don Bradley, David Brearey, Ron Carter, Tony Lato, Jesse Loucks, Ken Martin, Pam Morris, John Pletcher, Mark Schulkamp, Kathryn Toth, Janet Lennox Moyer

2012 Class 1 Brunswick, NY
Attendees: Jeff Calhoun, Mary Cutler, Patricia Dunn, Michael DuPont, Eddy Kyle, Renee Holzwarth, Kris Klein, Karen Libby, James Marshall, Tessa O'Regan, Tanya Pardo, Kyle Rehder, Katie Wilsey, Scott Williams; IALD Student Attendee: Haley Lawrence; Sponsor: Eric Beaudin, Aquasol Outdoor Lighting; Lead Mentors: Tony Lato, Jesse Loucks, John Pletcher; Instructors and Mentors: Don Bradley, David Brearey, Emily Gorecki, John KennyKen Martin, Chris Mitchell, Pam Morris, Jim Ply, Mark Schulkamp, Ken Simons, Paul Welty, Janet Lennox Moyer

2012 Class 2 Brunswick, NY
Attendees: Jon Adams, Lyle Braund, Clare Brew, Ryan Bushman, Anna Cheng, Franco D'Ascanio, John Gach, Ada Gates, Jon Carlo Marras, Neal David, Jordan Nodelman, Steve Prudhomme, Joel Reinders, Zach Rundle; IALD Student Attendee: Ute Besenecker; Lead Mentors: Tony Lato, Jesse Loucks, John Pletcher; Instructors and Mentors: Don Bradley, David Brearey, Heinrich Fischer, Carlton Hastings, Booth Hemmingway, Bob Isleib, Jack Magai, Arborist, Corey MacCallum, Ken Martin, Betsy Mitchell, Mark Schulkamp, Kathryn Toth, Tom Williams, Janet Lennox Moyer

2013 Brunswick, NY
Attendees: Carol Aronson, Matthew Broyles, Matt Bullard, Joe Daubel, Ramona Dimon, Elizabeth Donoff, Rene Gingras, Tommy Herren, Mike Holmes, Kris Horner, Susan Leaming Polish, Laurel Madden, Matt Moore, Jill Mulholland, Scott Shadwick, Jeremy Sviben, Scott Wilson, Corey Yourkin; Sponsors: Craig Klomparens and Woody Luke, Dauer LED; Lead Mentors: Ken Martin, Chris Mitchell, Bob Tubby; Instructors and Mentors: Darin Ayres, Don Bradley, David Brearey, Clare Brew, Eddy Kyle, Booth Hemingway, Rita Koltai, Cory MacCallum, Jim Ply, Mark Schulkamp, Kathryn Toth, Tom Williams, Scott Williams, Katie Wilsey, Janet Lennox Moyer; Class Support: Lisa Case, Stacey Fullova

2014 Class 1 Brunswick, NY
Attendees: Ryan Berrios, Tim Doogs, Kevin Fuscus, John George, Ryan Jasso, Henry T Johnson, Alex Lemieux, Will Lesieute, David Osborne, Alan Richmond, William Steinbrink, Ryan Williams, Brett Zimmerman; IALD Student Attendee: Apoorva Jalindre; Sponsor: Woody Luke, Dauer LED; Lead Mentors: Emily Gorecki, Chris Mitchell, Jim Ply; Instructors and Mentors: Don Bradley, David Brearey, Ron Carter, Rick Dekeyser, Ramona Dimon, Jesse Loucks, Brooke Perin, Mark Schulkamp, Brooke Silber, Scott Williams, Katie Wilsey, Janet Lennox Moyer; Class Support: Lisa Case, Marty Checci, Kathleen Hill

2014 Class 2 Brunswick, NY
Attendees: David Colborne, Will Irvin, Devon Jarvis, Shawn Knudson, Alanis Luciana, Jonathan Nastasia, Greg Ortt, David Reed, Todd Zimmerman; Sponsor: Woody Luke, Dauer LED; Lead Mentors: Betsy Mitchell, Chris Mitchell; Instructors and Mentors: Don Bradley, David Brearey, Mary Cutler, Eddie Kyle, Carlton Hastings, John Kenny, Tony Lato, Jesse Loucks, Mark Schulkamp, Kathryn Toth, Janet Lennox Moyer; Class Support: Lisa Case, Marty Checci, Brooke Silber, DeWitt Silber, Ken Silber

Teaching Via the Intensive Course International Landscape Lighting Institute
SECTION IV

Mockups and Installations – ILLI Class Photos

2015 Rio Verde, Arizona
Attendees: Devon Anastario, Jessica Collier, Angela Hall, Chip Israel, Anthony Italia, Tommy Johnson, Woody Kerwin, Travis Lerdahl, Bruce Pleckan, Nathan Sloane, Drew Tedford; Sponsors: Jerry Carter, Excelsior Lighting, Anna Cheng, HK Lighting Group, Zach Ingalls, Eaton/Cooper/Lumiere, Kris Klein, FX Luminaire, Nathan Sloane, BK Lighting/Teka; Lead Mentors: Emily Gorecki, Jesse Loucks, Betsy Mitchell, John Pletcher, Jim Ply, Instructors and Mentors: Mary Cutler, John Kenny, Tony Lato, Ken Martin, Ken Simons, Kathryn Toth, Scott Williams, Janet Lennox Moyer

2016 Ridgewood, NJ (no class photo - an action shot in the equipment garage)
Attendees: Ian Altares, Kaska Arencibia, Scott Armusewicz, Raul Avila, Brian Bunsch, Renee Byers, James Cervantes, Wes Jackson, Heather Libonati, Josh Miller, Brian Niles, Chris Olsen, Justin Perez, Carlos Ramirez, Darrin Schmuckle, Eric Schneider, Jordan Telford, Kellan Vincent; Lead Mentors: Emily Gorecki, Betsy Mitchell, Paul Welty, Instructors and Mentors: Don Bradley, David Brearey, Mary Cutler, Kevin Fuscus, John Kenny, Tony Lato, Jesse Loucks, Ken Martin, Brooke Perin, Bruce Pleckan, Andy Robbins, Mark Schulkamp, Brooke Silber, Bill Smith, Kathryn Toth, Scott Williams

2017 Tokamachi, Japan
Attendees from India, Japan, Thailand, USA: Yukari Atsuta, Nagisa Endo, Nilesh Kacheria, Chasiongkram Kaewngoen, Vida Khemachitphan, Haruki Kobayashi, Takatsugu Kamaki, Prapavee Kunuchit, Kinuyo Motohira, Tippaya Prasetsuk, Akiko Sakai, Yoshiko Soejima, Richard Wang; Lead Mentors: Jim Ply, Paul Welty; Instructors and Mentors: David Brearey, Wes Jackson, Jeff Kamm, John Kenny, Tony Lato, Karen Libby, Jesse Loucks, John Pletcher, Sarah Pletcher, Andy Robbins, Bill Smith, Kathryn Toth, Peeraanong Wongtanakomchai, Janet Lennox Moyer; Sponsor: Hiroshi Kira, HK Lighting Group, Ito and Reiko Ito, HK Lighting Group, Japan, Masaki Ito and Natsuko Takeda, Japan Lighting Coordinate Association; Interpreters: Adam Barnett, Sven Bjelan, and Joelle Limm, Tokamachi City International Relations; Joshua Frydman, University of Oklahoma, and Satoshi Suzuki, HK Lighting Group; Tokamachi City Officals and Local Residents who helped, lodged, and fed the design team (not all shown here, some in previous images): Yoshifumi Sekiguchi, Tokamachi City Mayor; Shigetoshi Kichira, Tokamachi City Regional Manager; Noboru Eguchi, Former Tokamachi City Regional Manager; Sone Atsushi, Naoko Takizawa, Abe Yoshinori, and Tomii Yoshiyuki Tokamachi City Officers; Toshiaki Takahashi, Kiyotsugawa Fresh Park Supervisor; Yutaka Eguchi, Yuki Hattori, Hideaki Nagumo, Kimiko Nagumo, Rie Nakai, Masashi Suzuki, Masako Takahashi, and Shoji Takahashi, Local Residents

2018 University of Oklahoma, Norman, Oklahoma
Attendees: David Evers, Kevin Fontaine, Greg Forsythe, Larry Gamer, Marc Haile, Mason Hancock, Patrick Harders, Scott Jackson, Brandon Kuehler, Chase Malibashka, Greg Matthews, Joel Mayor, Tim Parke, Wes Pederson, Ty Rosser, Rahul Sahu, Steve Schafer, Ryan Shoop, Matthew Wolff; Lead Mentors: , Jim Ply, Kathryn Toth, Paul Welty; Instructors and Mentors: Don Bradley, Wes Jackson, Jeff Kamm, John Kenny, Tony Lato, Jesse Loucks, John Pletcher, Scott Williams

2019 Rio Verde, Arizona
Attendees: Sadie Berg, Jamie Clarke, Chris Erca, Chris Graef, Christi Hamburger, Brad Homniok, Lezlie Johannessen, David Land, Jeff Marsh, Louis Martinez, Katy Moser, Kelly O'Connell, David Reed, Dayton Robinson, Mark Salopek, Andy Shumate, Travis Tabet, Marissa Tucci, Amy Weinberg; Lead Mentors: Emily Gorecki, Wes Jackson, Kathryn Toth; Instructors and Mentors: David Brearey, Rick Dekeyser, Dawn Hollingsworth, Jeff Kamm, Tony Lato, Janet Lennox Moyer, Jesse Loucks, Ken Martin, Greg Matthews, Chris Mitchell, Pam Morris, Jim and Stephani Ply, Mark Schulkakmp, Bill Smith

International Landscape Lighting Institute — Teaching Via the Intensive Course
SECTION IV
A Vintage, Intensive Course, Flyer

The Landscape Lighting Institute

A brief course description

The comprehensive landscape lighting experience with full-scale mockup of the Gardens at Dog Park using all major manufacturers equipment.

This course is open to students, landscape architects, landscape designers and all practicing professionals, includes: lectures on design and technical information specific to landscape lighting; afternoon design workshop sessions, and five nights of hands-on mockups. Learn the essentials of bringing your projects to life with well designed landscape lighting for maximum beauty and enjoyment. Expand your knowledge and income by adding this important field to your scope of work.

The emphasis of the course is a hand's-on experience to familiarize attendees with the equipment available on the market and the light source palette available to create lighting effects landscape spaces. Because landscape lighting differs dramatically from other areas of lighting design, the opportunity to work with lighting fixtures from all the major manufacturers will accelerate the attendees knowledge of lighting techniques. Seeing other designers' approaches also expands each persons palate of lighting effects.

Landscape lighting projects never end, as the landscape continually evolves. Jan will discuss the importance of planning infrastructure and lighting system flexibility from the beginning to respond to all the changes that landscape experience. She will also address conceptual through working drawings into record documentation. Jan will also cover the need for and how to plan and implement an on-going maintenance strategy. Don't miss this tremendous opportunity to learn from the industry's best.

Testimonials:

Life is much more exciting since my visit to Dog Park. The ideas, creativity, and possibilities are around every corner. Please tell Jan THANKS!
Rick Dekeyser class of 2007 - Key West

I want to thank you for all your hard work and your fantastic course! I have never learned so much in such a short time.
Jerry Carter class of 2008 - California

Jan & Team, I cannot stop thinking about the marvelous time I had at the Institute. It's nearly impossible to describe it….So full of ideas and inspiration in every session, WOW!
Oscar Welch class of 2008 - Florida

Jan, I want you to know that I have attended many national and regional conferences of all kinds over 35 years, but, I got the most out of yours.
Larry Iorii class of 2008 - Delaware

Thank you for creating a most exceptional experience! I leave the workshop with a much greater appreciation and passion for the power of light. The scenes and spaces created by all of the participants were truly works of art.
Paul Welty class of 2008 - Oregon

9780367193577